Bodyguard to Charles

Michael Varney
with Max Marquis

ROBERT HALE · LONDON

© *Michael Varney and Max Marquis 1989*
First published in Great Britain 1989

Robert Hale Limited
Clerkenwell House
Clerkenwell Green
London EC1R 0HT

British Library Cataloguing in Publication Data

Varney, Michael
    Bodyguard to Charles
    1. Great Britain. Charles, Prince of Wales,
    1948– Biographies
    I. Title   II. Marquis, Max
    941.085′092′4

ISBN 0–7090–3717–1

Set in Bembo by Derek Doyle & Associates, Mold, Clwyd
Printed in Great Britain by
St Edmundsbury Press, Bury St Edmunds, Suffolk
and bound by WBC Bookbinders

Bodyguard to
Charles

Contents

List of Illustrations

PICTURE CREDITS

BBC Hulton Picture Library: 1, 8; Popperfoto: 2; The Press Association: 9; Syndication International: 11.

Beginning and End

I was in the doghouse with Prince Charles – and literally so, for I was living in converted kennels at Gordonstoun School. It was clear that he wanted nothing to do with me. He was polite, of course, but formal and distant. In fact, in someone less well brought-up his deliberate coldness would be described as plain sulkiness.

I had worked hard to become a member of the Royal Protection Group of the Metropolitan Police. When I was told that I was to become the Prince's bodyguard I could scarcely believe my good fortune in achieving such an honour...and responsibility. But, almost at once, it all turned sour, and I wondered how long I should survive.

The Prince's studied indifference was not because of anything I had done. It was simply that he was badly upset that his previous bodyguard, Don Green, had been dismissed – unfairly, Charles believed, for something that wasn't Don's fault. Don had built up a relationship with the young Prince, who resented me for having taken his place.

Since we had both come to Gordonstoun I had spent my evenings in front of the television or reading, frankly bored and dejected at the way things had turned out. Then one night there was a soft tapping on my door. Prince Charles was paying me a first visit.

'I was wondering whether I could have a look at your television?' he said diffidently. His tone was quite different from anything I had heard before.

'Of course,' I said, trying not to sound elated.

He came and sat beside me, and we watched television together in silence. Then, very quietly, he asked me a question so poignant, so revelatory, that it shook me and gave me a sudden insight into the young Prince that I hadn't had before. From that moment on our relationship changed radically.

For nearly seven years I was with him more than any other adult, perhaps more than most fathers with their own sons, in his most relaxed and receptive moments. I look back at that period now with very mixed feelings, for only recently has it dawned on me just how close I was to the heir to the throne. Only now do I realize how important those formative years I spent at his side were to the future King Charles III.

When at last it was all over, the final parting seemed strangely unreal. As I exchanged the last goodbyes with Prince Charles in a quiet room at Buckingham Palace it was as if each of us had become a different person. We were almost strangers.

In the years when I had been close to him I had seen him change almost out of recognition. From a hesitant, shy, unworldly boy barely into his teens he had become an accomplished, self-confident – outwardly, at least – young man richly qualified to play his future role as king.

Throughout the years when I was Charles's shadow there were set-ups designed to trap him into embarrassing situations for the sake of a cheap headline...or worse. I managed to get him out of some of them only by the skin of my teeth. Some of them he never knew about until much later: perhaps he still doesn't to this day.

Charles himself had a great natural talent for getting himself into situations that were potentially highly embarrassing or even physically dangerous – through no fault of his own – which required very swift action. As his bodyguard, the man closest to him for twenty-four hours a day, I too was a target for people who wanted to get at the Prince for reasons of their own. More than once I was tricked into a situation which required all my ingenuity or determination to escape from. Or plain luck.

I suppose I must have done a reasonable job as his detective. When I was first assigned to him – the youngest officer ever to have that responsibility – I was told that in future all tours of duty with him would be for three months only. I was with him for nearly seven years, and I was told that he didn't want me to go when I was posted away.

Now at last the relationship which had effectively begun in a plainly furnished room in converted dog kennels was ending in the quiet luxury of a palace room. It was a difficult moment, for both of us. I learned a bitter lesson at that parting.

What was my reward for nearly seven years service to our future king?

Not promotion: I was still Police Constable Varney.

Not money: my last communication from the palace was a letter asking me to refund £3 overspent on my Christmas present of a pen.

My real reward was being close to Charles, Prince of Wales, watching him grow up, learning to respect and admire him for his sterling qualities and humour. And, in all honesty, *helping* him through those formative years.

1 The Long, Slow Road to Buckingham Palace

Norfolk is a pleasant county with rich soil that supports a thriving agricultural industry. It has one port in Great Yarmouth, and it is famous for its turkeys. However, it could hardly be called lively.

When I left school in 1955 I became a probationary policeman of the Norfolk County Constabulary at King's Lynn where I served for three years before being transferred to Hunstanton. While I was there I did have one notable report to make. It concerned the then Viscount Althorp – who, incidentally, had a daughter, Lady Diana Spencer, who was to become fairly well known. I reported the Viscount for 'failing to set a handbrake on a stationary vehicle'. His parked car rolled forward into another. Heady stuff.

From Hunstanton I was posted to Attleborough, a large village or small town of some 6,000 inhabitants. By the time I had been there three months I felt I knew every one of them. Lawbreaking was mostly on the level of poaching an odd pheasant or riding a bicycle without lights. Occasionally there was an exciting case of riding a bicycle in a reckless fashion.

One Attleborough builder actually 'stole' some of his own bricks to provoke a police response. As a ratepayer he felt he was entitled to see some action. Our local crime wave reached its peak just before Christmas, when turkey-rustlers from the towns might be about. There was no great market for sleeping pills in Attleborough.

When I was first sent to Sandringham to help with royal protection duties, it was as if a door had been opened onto another world. Almost immediately after I arrived I was determined to become a member of the Royal Protection Group. This was not because I had seen members of the royal family at close quarters, albeit fleetingly, or because they had said 'Good morning' or 'Good afternoon' to me personally as they passed one of the police posts on the estate. My only other contacts with members of the family were snowballs that were hurled at us by the mischievous Charles or Anne.

My motive was simply to get away from being a village bobby and to become a policeman in London – at Buckingham Palace in particular – and at Windsor, Balmoral and Edinburgh. That was the limit of my ambition. Perhaps even that was really too high an aim for a man who was described by one of his teachers as having two main failings: I was too honest and too careful, which would prevent my getting on in the world. My headmaster was even more disparaging. When I left school he told me bluntly: 'You'll be no use to man or beast.' The jury is still out on that one.

The problem was, I had to be in the Metropolitan Police to join the Group, and the Met had already turned me down once. As soon as I left school I applied to join the Met, took the entrance examination, but was rejected on medical grounds. I never knew what those grounds were.

Don Green, Prince Charles's detective at the time, had originally been a member of the Norfolk Constabulary like myself, stationed at Hunstanton. I asked his advice on getting a transfer to the Met, but he wasn't very helpful. At first I found this difficult to understand, for we were quite friendly; then I realized that he may have seen me as a threat to his own position. If I had thought of it at the time the possibility of my becoming Prince Charles's bodyguard would have seemed as likely as winning the pools or marrying Marilyn Monroe. Ironically, though, I was to take over from Don after a headline scandal.

It was George Murphy, one of the royal chauffeurs, who put me on the correct track. He told me that the best way – the only way – to become a member of the Royal Protection Group was to get the help of the Queen's detective, Chief

Superintendent Perkins, the head of the Group. And the best way to meet the august Mr Perkins (later Sir Albert Perkins MVO) was in off-duty hours at his favourite pub, The Feathers at Dersingham.

Whenever the royal family visited Sandringham the pub became quite busy. In addition to its regulars it was used by Household staff and by extra police drafted in from the surrounding countryside, which included me at the time. Although all other royal residences were guarded by the Metropolitan Police, for some reason Sandringham was always protected by local policemen. I never discovered for certain why this was so, but it was generally rumoured to have been George VI's tribute to the then Chief Constable for some service he had rendered the King.

The Feathers was a pleasant, homely pub with a large inglenook fireplace opposite the main bar. For the most part the regulars were local estate workers and village business people. However, when the royal family were at Sandringham for Christmas a number of customers from rather further afield used to turn up at the pub, presumably in the slender hope of seeing one of the royal family popping in for a quick one, although I can't remember any of them ever doing so.

Anyway, one evening I strolled into the pub when Perkins and Murphy were there. The conversation was opened with that great English universal introduction, 'What'll you have?' A few pints later Mr Perkins was telling me that if I really wanted to become a member of the Royal Protection Group I should apply for a transfer from the Norfolk Constabulary to the Met. When – if – I was in, I should telephone him at Buckingham Palace to remind him of our chat and he'd do what he could for me.

Maybe it was my youth that made me charge ahead optimistically after my previous rejection by the Met. Anyway, I told my Chief Constable that I wanted to transfer to the London Metropolitan Police, but I carefully avoided mentioning my eventual ambition of joining the Royal Protection Group.

The Chief Constable refused to allow me to apply for a transfer. At that time I assumed it was because the Norfolk force was under strength, and the Chief Constable presumably didn't want to lose another officer. I thought it was rather mean of him. I was impatient to get to London, but my countryman's natural caution made me decide to go along with the Chief Constable's suggestion. In fact, when the time came he allowed me to apply to join the Met before I resigned from the Norfolk Constabulary. I took the entrance examination again and was accepted this time. Not till then did I resign.

I'm sure that the Chief Constable made me follow this procedure in my own best interests, for I should still have a job with the county force if my attempt to get to London (and into the Royal Protection Group) fell flat.

The whole process was a drawn-out, tiresome affair. The ten months between my making the first move and finally arriving at Marylebone Lane Police Station, on 31 October 1960, were the longest I had known.

To learn about patrolling a beat I went out with another officer. I did it for just one day: my total experience of beat work in London. The next day I was posted to Peel House, off the Vauxhall Bridge Road, for training.

I spent much of my time between training-periods nipping in and out of telephone boxes trying to get into touch with Chief Superintendent Perkins at Buckingham Palace … without success. At the end of the second day at Peel House it suddenly dawned on me what I'd done. I'd resigned from my local force and come to the big city purely on the strength of a brief conversation in a pub ten months previously in which no hard promises were given. Chief Superintendent Perkins was a very senior officer and head of the Royal Protection Group, and his office was in Buckingham Palace: surely I could have confidence in such a solidly respectable figure? But quite unexpectedly the words of a psalm we learned in Sunday School came into my mind for the first time in goodness knows how many years: 'Put not your trust in princes….' In this case the 'prince' was the Chief Superintendent.

Even had Mr Perkins meant what he said at the time we met in the pub, there was a good chance that he no longer remembered that insignificant probationary constable of a country force. And if he did remember me, there might not be any jobs going in the Group anyway. That second night I lay awake feeling alternately angry and sorry for myself. The next day it came home to me how different the actuality was from the ambitions I'd had. I was going to pound London pavements in an unpleasant acrid atmosphere polluted by the smoky exhausts of buses and cars instead of in the clean air of my native Norfolk. I should have to deal with a public of total strangers, the majority of whom seemed to be at least slightly hostile to a police uniform. This whole situation was poles apart from my dream of strolling around palace gardens and country estates, keeping a watchful eye on members of the royal family.

The third day I did finally manage to get through to Mr Perkins. Despite the difference in our ranks I did most of the talking: I reminded him who I was, where we met, what we talked about and why I was in London. He replied as non-committally as a politician, and when I walked out of the telephone box I was aware that I was really no further forward than when I went into it. This second conversation had ended as inconclusively as the first.

Two days later, in the canteen, a colleague said to me 'You've only been here five minutes and I see you've already been posted to A Division.'

'No, I haven't,' I told him. 'Nobody's said anything.'

He passed over the latest Police Orders, something I'd never heard of before. He pointed to a line. There it was in black and white. I was posted to A Division, Cannon Row. All the clouds of doubt rolled away. The posting meant that all the nods and winks had registered, all the right strings had been pulled. Cannon Row is the station from which all officers on royal protection duties are drawn. As I walked out of Peel House it was all I could do to stop myself bursting into song. I was about to walk though the gates of Buckingham Palace for the first time.

This had hardly sunk in when I suffered a sudden reaction of disappointment. Here I was, a grandly titled Royal Protection Officer about to guard Buckingham Palace itself, yet it seemed that I had been selected as casually as a doorkeeper of a cinema. I felt let down that I hadn't been interrogated by MI5 and my loyalty thoroughly established. I was put through no special training; no one gave me any briefing for what struck me as highly important duties.

There was no word of small-arms practice. Nothing. But I would be guarding the *royal family*, for goodness sake! (Today security isn't taken quite as lightly as in that rather more casual period.)

In any case, I soon learned that my duties were far from sensitive or glamorous. My job was guarding one of the gates or tramping a beat round the palace forecourt. Were it not for where I was stationed, I told myself, my job would be less exciting than patrolling the Norfolk lanes by Attleborough. There was no escaping the fact that the job was more than a little boring. My major occupation was dealing with the endless crowds of visitors. There was always a fair proportion of people with one thought in mind: to get on the other side of the railings and closer to the palace building.

They had opportunities enough. Every time the policeman at the gate stepped out to hold up traffic and let an official car through the gate was unguarded. In the tourists scuttled. Rounding them up needed the skills and patience of a sheepdog. Fortunately many of them had cameras and stood still to aim them, which made them easier to collect.

Since those first days of duty at Buckingham Palace I have always admired the policeman on duty at the Members' entrance to the House of Commons, particularly after a general election, for he has to learn to recognize some 600-odd MPs at a glance. Learning the faces and names of the members of the royal Household caused me considerable problems. My biggest embarrassment was when I failed to recognize the Queen's Private Secretary. I stopped him when he was breezing through the North Centre Gate one morning and asked him to identify himself.

He told me who he was, without offering any identification.

'I'm sorry, sir,' I began, but he interrupted sharply,

'I am the Queen's Private Secretary and I don't have time to waste.'

I frankly didn't know quite what to do, and I just stood there, in his way. At last, giving me a look that I could feel burning right through to the back of my skull, he walked round me and on towards the palace.

'I shall report you to Mr Perkins,' he said with a voice like broken glass, and hurried off towards the Privy Purse.

I have to confess that at the time I was more afraid of what the formidable Mr Perkins might say to me than the possibility that I had let in a well-dressed anarchist posing as the Queen's Private Secretary. However, I heard nothing from the head of the Royal Protection Group, whatever report of my behaviour he might have been given from the tetchy private secretary. In fact I suspect that Mr Perkins might well have taken my side on principle.

When I joined the royal protection service I thought I had seen the last of late-night drunks, but patrolling the forecourt with a colleague one night we were frozen in our tracks by the sound of a man's loud, drunken singing echoing back from the walls of the palace. Very loud, very drunk. And his accent made it obvious that the reveller wasn't a member of the royal family. At least the gatecrasher wasn't singing a lewd song: he was roaring out 'Rule Britannia'. At first we couldn't see him, and when he paused for breath we didn't know which way to look. Then the uninvited visitor started up again with 'Land of Hope and Glory'. Well, at least he was patriotic.

My colleague and I homed in on the raucous singing and found a slumped figure sprawled spectacularly on the steps of the Grand Entrance with a couple of suitcases beside him, like a tourist who had arrived at his hotel too late and found it shut for the night. He was wearing a kilt and a pair of vivid red and green socks. Moving a deadweight drunk and a couple of suitcases would normally be something of a problem for two men, but the pair of us rushed him off the premises in record time, terrified that we would hear a window being opened and a voice demanding to know what was going on down there. We managed to get him outside without anyone inside the palace being any the wiser.

But how had the drunk and his suitcases got past the guard on the gate?

Then it occurred to us. Earlier that evening a taxi had driven up. When he got to the gate the driver wound down his window and asked the way to the Grand Entrance. I glanced at the seat at the back but there was no one in it, and my colleague and I assumed that the taxi had come to pick up a member of the royal Household coming off duty late. The drunk must have been lying on the floor of the cab. The driver probably thought it was a huge joke to deliver a drunk and his cases to the Grand Entrance of Buckingham Palace, but my fellow-PC and I swore that we'd do all sorts of unmentionable things to that driver if we ever saw him again.

Inevitably, routine duties at Buckingham Palace were fairly dull. Nights were even more boring and uneventful than days – apart from that one incident with the drunk. Although I was overjoyed when I was first posted to the palace, I soon became impatient to move on to something more interesting. Trying not too sound too pushy, I 'casually' asked some of my more experienced colleagues how long a constable usually served as an ordinary palace beat policeman before being given the responsibility of protecting a particular member of the royal family. I could look forward to six months of the usual dull, routine duties, I was told. Well, patience is a virtue you have to learn in the police. It took me ten months to get from Norfolk to Buckingham Palace. I could stick it out for a few more months until I moved on to something more lively than patrolling the same old forecourt. I didn't even have to patrol the high-walled grounds, which look impressive in built-up London but are only about 500 yards by 500 yards. Every day I was there the grounds seem to shrink a little more.

Nevertheless, we managed to relieve the boredom of night duty from time to time. One of our major distractions was our private 'flapping track' – slang for an unlicensed dog-racing track. At night we were usually joined by two dog-handlers with their Labradors. The breed is not renowned for its speed, but police Labradors are well-trained, amiable and willing creatures. In silence the duty dogs cheerfully raced each other along the terraces, carrying a few modest bets on them. They probably enjoyed the activity just as much as we did.

There was another regular distraction, although the principal character in it intended to be anything but amusing. When the Court was away from the palace the Resident Police Inspector would often take the opportunity to catch up on his back leave. While he was away his duties were taken over by an officer from Cannon Row Police Station. One inspector in particular was zealous to the point of obsession in trying to catch us in such infractions as not being alert enough, taking an extra five minutes for a tea-break or having a surreptitious smoke in some quiet corner on night duties. His favourite approach was to let himself in by the gate near the Wellington Arch, and creep round the lake and across the lawn to the terrace to see what regulations we were breaking.

He must have been a very frustrated man. Not once did he catch us in the least misdeed of commission or omission. This wasn't because all the policemen on duty were model officers incapable of any trifling misdemeanour. The explanation was much simpler. As soon as the inspector set out from Cannon Row our colleagues telephoned to warn us he was on his way. So he regularly found a smart, alert set of policemen on duty.

For the most part we found the officer's activities mildly amusing, but after a while his snooping began to irritate us, and we decided to do something about it. One night he was making his secretive way across the dark lawn when a Labrador shot out from some bushes and with a mighty bound sent him sprawling in a muddy, undignified heap. A dog handler had been waiting in ambush, and as soon as the inspector came into sight the handler whispered 'Fetch!' to the dog, who must have been delighted to have something positive to do for a change.

The dog was called off the prostrate figure and the inspector was allowed to get up and establish his identity. It's certain that he wasn't fooled by the po-faced, effusive apologies that were heaped on him by a group of other constables who suddenly appeared on the scene. In any case, that was the last of his would-be clandestine night visits. I think we actually missed him after a while.

Almost as irritating as the earnest inspector were, I regret to say, the royal corgis. For those not used to them they can be alarming little animals, for they have a tendency to snap. The royal ones were probably more aggressive than most, for they virtually had a licence to bite without fear of retribution, which encouraged them...except on one occasion. One evening a fellow-constable gave a yelp as one of the dogs nipped him painfully on the ankle. Instinctively he gave it a boot up the backside. All at once he realized what he had done – practically committed an act of *lèse-majesté*. He looked round but there was no one in sight.

The next morning there was a polite royal request – which ranked as an order – to refrain from kicking the dogs, whatever the provocation. Murphy's Law had operated: at that one brief moment when the policeman had booted the dog, the Queen had been looking out of her window.

Then at last I was assigned the first of my plain-clothes duties of escorting the royal children on their trips away from the palace.

2 The Small Royals

Although I did occasional duties with younger members of the royal family, my first regular outings were with Prince Andrew. It was a good way to break me in to royal protection duty, because even the second in the line to the throne isn't all that awe-inspiring at the age of three. Andrew was simply a lively, rather well-dressed and well-spoken child. Besides, we were always accompanied by one of those most formidable of creatures who brook no nonsense from anyone, including Princes of the Blood: an experienced British nanny.

Andrew's weekly treat was a visit to Paddington Station to watch the trains. I remembered reading somewhere before we had the outings that there were many very ordinary things that members of the royal family could never enjoy. One was that they couldn't travel on a bus like everyone else. Well, Prince Andrew managed it and enjoyed it hugely. We always went to Paddington on the top deck of a bus. It was a mixed pleasure for me, for each time I had to try to talk the conductor into parting with a whole roll of tickets. The ticket machine fascinated Andrew even more than the trains.

One afternoon as we were preparing to get off the bus I picked up Prince Andrew in my arms to carry him downstairs. I bumped his head on the roof. He took it well and made no fuss but a lady sitting opposite us said in a loud voice, 'Really, some fathers have no idea how to look after their children.'

I didn't have time to think about what the woman had said

until we were in Paddington Station and Andrew was bubbling with pleasure at watching the trains arriving and departing. I suddenly realized – for the first time: it was to come back to me a hundred times again – that there are many other homely, ordinary things, too, that members of the royal family can never know. These trips to watch the trains that Andrew made with me were the sort of outings that parents take their kids on themselves, not have to send them with the hired help.

Andrew was a marvellous child to be with, but like all children he could sometimes cause embarrassment to the adults with him. And because of his position, his potential for making heads turn was considerable. On an occasion when we returned from a morning train-spotting trip to Paddington we stopped outside the palace railings to watch the Changing of the Guard. I lifted him onto my shoulders so he could get a good look over the heads of the tourists. It was a new point of view for him at ground-level, of course, because he normally watched the ceremony from above, at the nursery window. Nobody took any notice of us until he said in a voice that carried:

'I do like Mummy's soldiers!'

('Mummy's soldiers'! What a way to describe the Brigade of Guards!) There was a sort of mass double-take, then all heads turned towards us, followed by a general buzz and 'Ooooh, look!' We'd been spotted. We hurried in through the gate to the palace side of the railings.

In some quite young children you can see the adult they will grow up to be. The mischievous Prince Andrew was one of those children. One of my regular outings with him was to Richmond Park, accompanied by Nanny Mabel Anderson. The excursions were a sort of get-together of certain top nannies and their young charges. They were quite delightful afternoons for anyone who loves children. These days it seems quite extraordinary that a young prince could go rushing around in a public park with only one unarmed detective to protect him. Of course, he was so young that not many people recognized him.

I used to keep the children amused while Mabel and the other nannies exchanged nursery secrets and, I've no doubt, gossip about 'their' children's parents. It doesn't take a great deal to amuse children: Andrew's and his companions' sport was to kick a ball about with enormous vigour but little skill.

One afternoon we were playing by Pen Ponds, which are near White Lodge, the home of the Royal Ballet School, and King George V Plantation, although I was unaware of the name at the time. The Plantation is divided by a path from Spankers Hill Wood, which is a name to cause some speculation. One of Andrew's friends gave the ball an unexpectedly powerful kick, and it went into the pond. I found a stick somewhere and tried to recover the ball but it kept bobbing away. I was leaning forward as far as I dared and was just about to get the ball under control when I felt a small nudge in the back.

What I should have done, of course, was to cut my losses and take a pace forward into the pond, recovering my balance at the small price of a soaked foot. Instead of which I tried to straighten up without moving my feet, my arms whirling like a couple of mad windmills. I suppose I must have looked like something out of a Harold Lloyd film.

I fell forward at full length, arms stretched out in front of me, into the shallow water at the edge of the pond. The front half of me was soaked from head to toe. I lay there for a moment, cursing silently so I shouldn't shock young ears. I scrambled up and turned round. Four small boys, all in a line, were regarding me with wide, innocent eyes. A fifth boy was looking very satisfied with himself, a smile lurking at the corners of his mouth while he glanced sideways at his companions, seeking their approval and admiration. Prince Andrew. It took no great feat of detection to work out who had pushed me.

I squelched away from the edge of the pond towards Nanny Anderson, to tell her we were going home. Unthinkingly she asked the question that most people would have asked: 'Did you fall in?'

She rounded up Andrew and prepared to leave with us.

As we moved off Andrew asked me, 'What about our ball?'

There was no answer to that. At least, not one I could give a young prince.

Once I started actually escorting members of the royal family – albeit the most junior ones at first, Andrew and then

Princess Anne – outside the palace on my own, I was given special training for the first time since the day I first walked through the palace gates.

I was given firearms practice.

This sounds impressive, but my entire training consisted of two hours' instruction at Finsbury Police Station. After I fired ten rounds the instructor could find only a single hole in the target. I failed to convince him that all the bullets had gone through the same hole. In the whole of my ten years' service with the Royal Family that was the only contact I ever had with a handgun. This rather casual approach to the carrying of arms at that time was encouraged by a history of forty years without any sort of attack on any member of the royal family. The foreign security men I came into contact with found it almost impossible to credit that Royal Protection Group officers were unarmed. On one occasion I was on duty in the grounds of Buckingham Palace during the visit of the late President Kennedy. I was approached by one of his security men from the so-called Secret Service, who asked my what type of gun I carried. I pointed two fingers at him and said, 'You're dead!'

He shook his head and wandered off, muttering, with a total lack of sincerity in his tone, 'That's what I like about you British. You've got such a great sense of humour.'

Of course, after the attempted armed kidnap of Princess Anne and Captain Phillips in The Mall in March, 1974, security became much tighter and more realistic.

I first met Princess Anne when she was about ten years old. With some carefully selected friends she was having lessons in the royal nursery from the late Miss Catherine Peebles, who was known to all the royal children as 'Mispy'. Under her enthusiastic guidance Anne and her two friends began a series of visits to such obvious tourist attractions as Westminster Abbey, the Tower of London, the Bank of England, and a number of museums, theatres and cinemas. I accompanied them as protection officer. These trips usually went unnoticed by the general public, even though we were a fairly large party. In addition to Princess Anne were 'Mispy', myself and two of Anne's classmates at Buckingham Palace, Susan ('Suki') Babbington-Smith and Caroline Hamilton. Even at this early age Anne showed clearly what sort of young woman she would grow up to be: her character was forthright and uncomplicated. (I was to find that Prince Charles was a much more complex and less revealing youngster. In the early stages of being with him it wasn't easy to predict what sort of man he would become.) One of Anne's most developed traits was her knowledge of what she wanted and her determination to get it. She so enjoyed the *Black and White Minstrel Show* at the Victoria Palace that she insisted on our all going again at least twice more. It was there, too, that she demonstrated her straightforwardness. She was fascinated to see how the artistes could move actively around the stage and yet never be out of breath when singing. When the technique of pre-recording and miming was explained to her, although she said it was a clever idea I could see she thought it was something of a cheat.

She was always the first to ask questions on subjects that interested her but made no polite attempts to hide her boredom when she found a subject tedious. On one occasion we visited the Bank of England where the ten-year-old Princess was met by the Governor. We were shown gold ingots piled high to the ceiling...millions and millions of pounds'worth. I came out in a cold sweat just to be near so much wealth. All that *gold!* But Anne made it plain that she wasn't in the least impressed, and said so. She asked our guide to take us back to the cable office – as it was then – where cables were coming in, moving vast sums of money back and forth across the world. It occurred to me later that money has little meaning for the members of the royal family. If they want something, they can have it without a second thought; 'cost' is a word that has little meaning to them. They don't even carry money around with them – as I found out to my cost and embarrassment some time later with Prince Charles.

Although we all went to musicals such as the *Minstrels*, and to pantomimes, ice shows, gymkhanas and other entertainments, most of our visits were purely educational, like the one to the Bank of England. When we did go to an entertainment 'Mispy' and I booked the tickets between us, as I have said, so that the visits would be largely unremarked. Going for the tickets also gave me the opportunity to have a good look round the area before our party went there.

Princess Anne had a fiercely competitive spirit even as a young girl – especially for one whose position meant that she never had to compete. She won her first rosette at the Hunter Trials at Binfield in April 1962. She came second on Bandit, which I thought was pretty good for a beginner, but as she collected the blue runner-up's rosette it was clear that it wasn't good enough for her. As far as she was concerned there was first place, and after that, nothing.

The strength of Anne's character was evident during another of her favourite pastimes: ice-skating. I accompanied her on regular visits to Richmond Ice Rink, where she skated on a small rink used for private lessons, away from the large one open to the general public. Our party – which usually consisted of Anne, her friends 'Suki' and Caroline, 'Mispy' and myself – were admitted a few minutes before the official opening time, so hardly any of the public knew we were there.

Anne had marvellous instructors: the world-famous Arnold Gerschweiler and his then assistant Betty Calloway, who later coached Torvill and Dean, among others. Like most beginners Anne spent more time sitting down than on her feet in the early stages. The determined and courageous way she struggled to her feet and battled on after every fall impressed even her instructors. One of them once told me that she was one of the most fearless pupils they had ever taught. Even allowing for a certain exaggeration on their part because of Anne's position, it was a handsome compliment. Perhaps her experiences in coming a cropper on the ice with a resounding bump stood her in good stead for her later horse-riding...

I saw a great deal of Princess Anne at this time, and it seemed to me that she was determined almost to the point of obsession to get as much as possible out of life before the chains of position and public duty prevented her from doing as much as she would like.

There was a period in later life when Princess Anne acquired a less than flattering public image: many people thought that she lacked a sense of humour and had an overdeveloped sense of her own importance. Perhaps she did over-react to the heat of the permanent spotlight that is directed onto all members of the royal family, but her every word and gesture was under the microscope of media attention. However, one of her many outstanding characteristics when she was a young girl was her strong sense of humour, both broad and subtle. It was the sort of sense of humour that was bound to prevail in the end so that she became once more the likeable young woman – although she suffered fools badly – that the young girl had foreshadowed.

From a purely personal point of view it was fascinating for me to me to watch this unique young family growing up, but at the same time all the outings with them had their particular problems. Then, as later when I became Prince Charles's protection officer, I always tried as much as possible to go beforehand and look at the places we were going to visit, as I had while accompanying Princess Anne. If I knew the topography of a building or a particular area I could work out possible escape routes if necessary. This was not for fear of potential assassins but simply to avoid being caught up in crowds if the young Royal was noticed, or simply in case there was a traffic jam or a fire or a demonstration of some sort. A cry of 'Oh, look, there's Prince So-and-so!' would cause a crowd to gather more quickly than scattering handfuls of Smarties in a kindergarten.

Then came the famous, or notorious, incident of Prince Charles and the cherry brandy.

I had escorted the young Prince on a few outings in and out of London when his regular detective, Don Green, was on leave, but it never occurred to me that I should take over from him one day – certainly not in the abrupt, unexpected and unpleasant way things turned out. It is with some reluctance that I bring up the subject because I know it caused Prince Charles bitter resentment for years and I shouldn't be surprised if it still does. However, there have been a number of imaginative and inaccurate accounts about the affair, and I think the record should be put straight. The real story underlines the difficulties of royal security, and at the same time gives some insight into the attitudes of Prince Philip and Chief Superintendent Perkins, and a first glimpse of the young Prince Charles's character.

In the summer of 1963 Charles was sailing in the Gordonstoun School schooner *Pinta* with Don Green and four other boys on a study exercise when it put into the harbour at Stornaway in the Outer Hebrides, a port of some 5,000 inhabitants. Don Green travelled directly there from Gordonstoun and arranged for Prince Charles and the other boys on the ship to have a meal in a private room at the local hotel. From there the party was going on to see a Jayne Mansfield film, presumably to study topography.

When the *Pinta* docked Green met the boys and led them to the hotel from the quay. At the hotel he was still in the lead. He took the party through the main door, past the bars and to the private room.

This was the first mistake in a whole series of mistakes and unhappy coincidences. When you are guarding someone and are responsible for his safety it is elementary that you must not let him out of your sight. The situation was not unlike escorting a prisoner: you never let him get behind you where you can't see him. (In fact, it was very like guarding a prisoner. Prince Charles and his brothers and sister are very much prisoners of their position. They can go out only rarely without their 'warders'; and if someone like Princess Diana is thought to get out of Buckingham Palace without her police guard it's front-page news, like a story of a prisoner escaping.)

The hotel was unusually crowded because the word had gone round that Charles was arriving. As he entered everyone turned and stared at him, which made him embarrassed and flustered. After all, he was only thirteen years old and he had lived a sheltered and restricted life. His lack of worldliness – even for a thirteen-year-old – was extreme, as was to be brought home to me later on more than one occasion.

All alone the Prince marched into the bar and ordered a cherry brandy. He asked for this rather unusual drink – particularly before lunch! – because he'd been given some when he went out shooting on cold days at Sandringham. It wasn't that he wanted a drink. He was simply trying to be grown-up and to do the right thing. Normally this would all have been seen for what it was and the whole petty incident quietly buried and forgotten. They say that you can never find a policeman when you want one; conversely, you can always find a journalist when you don't. As ill-luck would have it on this day there was a woman reporter in the bar:

twenty-two-year-old Frances Thornton, a freelance journalist. Anyway, Charles paid his half-a-crown (12½p) for the cherry brandy and sipped it. The reporter couldn't have believed her luck: a marvellous story of the under-age heir to the throne ordering hard liquor in a bar!

As soon as she phoned her story to her office the newspaper immediately phoned the press officer at Buckingham Palace. The obvious reply was 'No comment': the story could be neither confirmed nor denied. The Palace, of course, immediately contacted Gordonstoun School, but they couldn't help either as the alleged incident – it was still 'alleged' at that point – had happened at Stornaway.

Bob Whitby, Prince Charles's housemaster at Gordonstoun, finally managed to get in touch with Don Green. At the end of their conversation Bob Whitby had the impression that nothing had happened. This is what the palace were told, and the press office issued an official denial. So, the newspaper called the journalist, who unhesitatingly – and correctly – confirmed her story. She was in the fortunate position of having several witnesses in the bar who could substantiate her account.

All this finally got back to the palace press office, and the official denial had to be withdrawn and the cherry brandy incident confirmed. There were a lot of red faces about the place, and a neck had to be found for the chopping- block. As is so often the case in this sort of affair, the blame always trickles down to the lowest level. Don Green was the victim. Prince Philip insists on truthfulness among palace staff, and he was adamant that Don had to go. Pleas from Bob Whitby and others – not least Prince Charles himself – were rejected. The Duke of Edinburgh wanted Don dismissed then and there, but eventually it was decided that he should stay until the end of that term so as not to disrupt Charles's studies too seriously.

There was a strong whiff of hypocrisy about the whole affair, for I learned later that it was far from unusual for Gordonstoun boys to have a drop of something when they came ashore from a sea trip. It was perhaps Charles's first lesson in how very differently from ordinary people the Press would treat him.

Looking back, I think Don was treated much less than

generously, and above all should have been firmly defended by Perkins, but the head of the Royal Protection Unit was very much an Establishment man. He wouldn't have wanted to make ripples, let alone waves.

The fact that Charles and the others were on the *Pinta* kept the incident alive. At the time there was an advertising campaign for milk with the ungrammatical but arresting slogan 'Drinka Pinta Milka Day'. (English teachers hated it.) When people punningly connected the name *Pinta* with cherry brandy everyone saw the joke....except Charles. I once tried to jolly him out of it, but it was quite hopeless: he closed up completely and I was afraid I had set back our relationship by some weeks. I never tried it again.

Soon after this incident Chief Superintendent Perkins took me aside and told me unofficially that I should be Prince Charles's next protection officer. It was the Assistant Commissioner 'A' ('Administration') who told me officially that I was to be Prince Charles's next protection officer. I was slightly apprehensive but, curiously enough, not over-excited; I was honoured but not over-awed by the prospect at the time. After all, I had been looking after Princess Anne and Prince Andrew for a couple of years, and I had even been relief officer taking care of Charles on a few occasions.

One of these had been during the Prince's visit to the Ministry of Defence's FVRDE – Fighting Vehicles Research and Development Establishment – at Chobham. Charles was accompanied by one of his German cousins who was at Gordonstoun with him, and the tour was conducted by Brigadier McKenzie. Although it was only a couple of days from June, the weather was depressing, with heavy rain just before our arrival.

Of course, the two boys were thrilled to be able to get into a tank and be taken for a ride. Charles, at least, had a boy's natural enthusiasm for a lifesize mechanical toy and seemed interested in the tanks. However, I had the strong impression that he wasn't all that taken by the thought that they were purely instruments of destruction.

The boys scrambled in excitedly through the hatches, which had been left open and the bucket seats covered to prevent their getting wet. Unfortunately the seat covers hadn't been removed from the tank I got into, and without looking I sat in a pool of water. I've no doubt that Charles and his cousin did the same. The rest of the day was miserable as I squelched around with a soaking wet patch in my trousers. You simply cannot have any dignity in that situation. Still, I wasn't as wet as when Prince Andrew had tipped me into the pond at Richmond Park. I was glad enough to return to duty with Princess Anne on a trip to a gymkhana at Woolhampton, near Newbury, the following day.

Because of my familiarity with being with members of the royal family, often in mundane circumstances, at the moment I was told of my appointment to be Charles's protection officer it did not seem all that meaningful that I was to be given the honour and responsibility of guarding the future king. On several occasions much later the weight of that responsibility was to hit me so hard that it was like a blow to the solar plexus.

A fortnight after seeing the Assistant Commissioner I went with Chief Superintendent Perkins to Gordonstoun to get to know the area and to meet the staff who were there at the time. That same day I returned to Balmoral and continued with uniformed duties there. Then another officer, David Groves, who was assigned to Princess Anne's protection, and I were called into Perkins's office at Balmoral for a final briefing.

Now, I thought, at last I'm going to be briefed on the vital details of protecting the heir to the throne. In fact, Perkins limited himself to the one and only piece of advice he ever gave me.

'If ever I ask for details of any incident, I want direct answers.' Any attempt on my part to lie or prevaricate would mean the equivalent of my being banished to pounding a beat in Outer Mongolia.

A trial run was decided on to see how Prince Charles and I got on together, although it was obvious that exercise of any choice would be pretty one-sided if it were up to the young Prince, for Charles was still deeply upset at what he considered to be the injustice of the sacking of his long-time friend and confidant Don Green. I was detailed to accompany Charles on a weekend fishing trip to the residence of the Dowager Duchess of Devonshire at Fochabers, a large

Morayshire village of some 1,200 inhabitants on the River Spey.

At first he flatly refused to go. Prince Philip would have none of it. He told Charles that I would be the officer returning to Gordonstoun with him, and it was time for Charles to grow up, behave like a man and accept things as they were and not as he would wish them to be. When the chauffeur-driven car left Balmoral Castle Charles waved goodbye to his parents, a white handkerchief in his hand, choking back tears. I couldn't help thinking that, for all the enormous wealth and influence of his family, despite all the comfort and freedom from fear of want he would always have, the thirteen-year-old Prince's life wasn't all that enviable. One of the few people with whom he had established some sort of relationship had been banished without appeal, and now this small boy was being packed off with a stranger to spend a weekend in an adult world away from home. And it was a grim weekend: to use one of Charles's own favourite words of the time, it was 'gruesome'. He ignored me: we exchanged no words that were not absolutely essential.

At another time I might have enjoyed the trip. Fochabers is an attractive place, and although it is quite small, it is famous out of all proportion to its size for being the home of Baxter's soups and jams. The salmon fishing in the Spey, so I am told, is excellent. It must have been of some consolation to the disconsolate young Prince, for he was – and still is, by all reports – an accomplished fisherman with a natural instinct for the sport. However, the weekend did nothing to lighten his resentment at Don Green's departure. He was still moody and uncommunicative when we went back to Balmoral where he was going to prepare for the rigours of his return to Gordonstoun. My own mood was as overcast as Charles's. I had looked forward to the moment when I would have my 'own' Royal to look after, but the whole thing had turned sour. There was another aspect of my appointment which troubled me. I was being given the responsibility of guarding our next king, yet his parents had not seen me, except at a distance or in passing, and had not interviewed me. I had to assume that they had accepted Chief Superintendent Perkins's recommendation of me as sufficient.

However, there was one examination I did have to undergo before my appointment as Prince Charles's detective was finally confirmed: a driving test. This was considered necessary because at Gordonstoun I should be driving the Prince in the Land Rover provided for him. The test was totally in keeping with the whole process of my selection and appointment up to then: casual almost beyond belief. I solemnly drove Harry Purvey, the Queen's head chauffeur, and Chief Superintendent Perkins in the Land Rover along the south Deeside road to Ballater, then back to Balmoral along the north Deeside road. In the whole sixteen-odd miles I don't think I had to change down into third gear more than once. There was no traffic, no junctions, not a single wobbly cyclist or even a stray lamb. It would have been difficult to fail me after a test like that.

Apart from this moment of wry light relief, I was feeling pessimistic about the future. If Charles's attitude to me didn't change the whole exercise of my being his bodyguard was going to end in dismal failure. I realized that his continued reaction to Don Green's dismissal proved that he was capable of strong loyalties. (This whole episode was brought back to me sharply when I read recently that Prince Charles had decided to have his son William's detective replaced by another officer – reportedly much to Prince William's active discontent. I suppose that Charles was only too aware of the bond that can be formed between a young boy and his constant companion, his detective. Since I was Charles's detective for 6½ years, I wonder how much he came to rely on me without my realizing it.)

At the time when I was appointed to be his protection officer it did not occur to me that I should have to earn the sort of trust that Don Green had enjoyed...and earn it the hard way.

When that thought finally did dawn I had to ask myself whether I should be capable of it.

Abruptly I was aware for the first time of my own youth and inexperience. I was untrained and only twenty-two-years old (I was the youngest officer ever to be assigned to Prince Charles)...and responsible for the safety of the heir to the throne.

3 Gordonstoun

The estate and big house of Gordonstoun have a long and rich history. The first recorded owner of the estate died in 1240, although it is probable that it had already been in the family for some time. The house itself really dates from about 1616, and to a great extent was the work of the first Marquess and sixth Earl of Huntly, George Gordon, one of the great builders of his age, although it has been extended by the later Gordons. The name of 'Gordonstoun' dates from about 1638, when Sir Robert Gordon, first Baron Gordonstoun, bought the estate and named it after himself.

One of the most interesting features of the Gordonstoun buildings is the Round Square, constructed by the third baronet in the 1690s. He was known as 'Sir Robert the Wizard' because of his scientific experiments, and for other, darker reasons. 'The Square' is the name traditionally given to the auxiliary buildings of a Scottish estate, for the simple reason that they were usually laid out in a square, but the Wizard designed his buildings in a circle of reputedly magical proportions. According to legend the reason was that Sir Robert had sold his soul to the Devil in exchange for exotic powers, and he wanted a retreat where the Devil could not catch him in a corner when he came to claim his soul. The legend continues that at the fateful moment of settlement Sir Robert changed his mind and rushed off to seek refuge in Birnie Kirk, one of the smallest but oldest of Scottish churches. Unfortunately the Devil was quicker than Sir Robert and nabbed him before he could get to Birnie.

Whatever the weight of the legend, it is factual that Sir Robert converted one of the vaults of Gordonstoun, the main building of the estate, into a workshop and laboratory. This is the room that has been used for years as a bathroom by Gordonstoun pupils.

The inspiration for Gordonstoun School was one founded by Prince Max of Baden at Salem in southern Germany after World War I. His private secretary, Kurt Hahn, was made Salem's first headmaster. Hahn was an admirer of certain aspects of English public schools; he was strongly influenced by the famous Dr Arnold of Rugby and by Plato. Admission to Salem was highly selective. Pupils were accepted only from the German upper classes, and character was much more important that mere academic ability.

Hahn was Jewish, so when Hitler came to power the school was closed and Hahn sent to prison. Released at last, he came to Britain where William Calder and Evan Barron, contemporaries of Hahn when he was a Rhodes Scholar at Oxford, helped him establish a school at Gordonstoun in 1934. That first year there were just thirty pupils, of whom one was Prince Philip of Greece, as today's Duke of Edinburgh was then.

Although Gordonstoun stemmed from the roots of Salem, Hahn placed much more emphasis on physical activities and the development of a boy's self-reliance and sense of duty to others. The school's motto is 'Plus est en vous' – 'There is more in you'. The preoccupation with physical activities is shown only too clearly by the boys' daily timetable.

At 7 a.m. the boys were roused by shouts of 'Waker!' As soon as they were sufficiently conscious, the majority of them prayed that the weather was bad, otherwise the next call was 'Morning run!' If rain was pelting down, there came the welcome 'No morning run'.

I disliked the boys' early morning run almost as much as they did. Occasionally I took part myself – very occasionally. More often than not I drove the Land Rover and took short cuts to intercept the runners along the course. Fortunately the morning runs and punishment runs were held within the extensive school grounds, so there was very little potential danger to Prince Charles. Still duty was duty and I had to put in some sort of appearance, which sometimes bordered on the purely token. The only threats to our peace of mind came from the odd hopeful journalist, but these attempted intrusions were usually coped with fairly easily. After the run the boys washed with hot water, following this with the first of the day's two cold showers. Then Charles, in common with the other boys, had to make his bed and clean his shoes before breakfast at 8.15. 'Surgery' (sick parade) was next.

There were prayers at 8.55 a.m., and at 9.10 a.m. classwork began. There were five forty-minute periods, but one would be a PT session ranging from running and jumping to an assault course supervised by the physical training master.

Lunch was at 1.20 p.m., and after that came a period of some twenty minutes relaxation lying down. This was accompanied by music or a reading out loud.

Afternoon activities began at 2.30 p.m.. There were competitive games on three afternoons a week, with one afternoon spent participating in one of the school's practical activities. These were Coast Guard Watching, Fire-Fighting, Mountain Rescue and Ocean Rescue – all efficient operational services which were called out in cases of emergency locally. Charles opted for coast-watching, which may sound like a fairly sedentary occupation, but it was far from that, for it involved clambering up and down cliff faces on ropes and rope ladders. Charles teamed up with his cousin Guelf to form a life-saving unit. They were awarded their proficiency certificates on his fourteenth birthday. Charles also enjoyed sailing, although his early experiences of sea-sickness were discouraging.

Dr Hahn instituted the Moray Badge as a mark of distinction in the service activities. The badge was the inspiration for the later Duke of Edinburgh Awards.

To return to the boys' very full programme: another afternoon and evening a week were devoted to work on their individual projects which were exhibited and judged at the end of each year.

Among other things Charles did pottery as a project, and at one exhibition he had five pieces on show. They were :

1. Dark blue on olive green pot
2. Pale green posy bowl and stand
3. 'The Quintet'
4. Golden brown flower pot holder
5. 'Fledgling'

On Saturday afternoons there were more matches or

expeditions.

At 4.00 p.m. was another warm wash and cold shower, and the boys changed into the school's evening uniform. After tea there were further classes or tutorial periods. Supper was at 6.20 p.m., followed by evening preparation. Bedtime was at what seemed to me at first an extraordinarily early time of 9.15 p.m., but I soon discovered that at night all life at Gordonstoun and in the surrounding countryside went into suspended animation.

So that I should know at all times where Charles was – or was supposed to be – on the large Gordonstoun estate he provided me with a timetable for the week.

For all Dr Hahn's progressive and advanced ideas, I couldn't help thinking that the morning run, stripped to the waist, and cold showers were old-fashioned ideas rather than modern ones. They smacked of the philosophy that cold showers and a couple of turns round the playing fields would help keep growing boys' minds off sex. As if anything could…!

Perhaps the diet was meant to do that. At the time the amount spent on food for each boy was 1s.9d. a day (8p. in today's money). Even taking into account the increased cost of living, it seemed a pretty frugal allowance for boys who were having so much physical activity.

I usually took my own meals in Gordonstoun House, in the masters' dining-room. It could not be mistaken for the Savoy Grill, and I occasionally topped up my calory count with beans on toast prepared in my own quarters. If I missed a meal for any reason, I couldn't just pop across the road to a burger bar or fried chicken takeaway: there simply wasn't one for miles. The fact that Charles had his detective on the premises didn't help him if he felt peckish in the night: I couldn't provide him with midnight snacks or spare nosh.

The boys all wore shorts with a single back pocket. No matter how big a pupil was, he never wore long trousers – not even the older boys who obviously shaved occasionally and had baritone voices. Shirts and V-necked sweaters completed the outfits. Boys changed into different coloured sets of the uniform according to the time of day and the season of the year. In winter they wore duffle coats with purple and white scarves when they moved around outside between classrooms. School books were carried in a canvas bag.

Prince Charles's return to, and my arrival at, Gordonstoun in the autumn of 1963 couldn't have been more unpromising. The place was always windy and cold, despite its local reputation for having an easier climate than the rest of the general area. Aircraft from RNAS Lossiemouth were always roaring overhead: sometimes it seemed that the school was at the end of the runway.

Charles was one of the sixty pupils who lived in Windmill Lodge, with Bob Whitby as his housemaster. The Lodge, an uninviting stone structure with an asbestos roof, was one of the subsidiary buildings some distance from the imposing main house. Like all the buildings in the Gordonstoun complex, it was anything but luxurious, with long, uncarpeted dormitories that had little heating and no lampshades. The sixty boys had one bath and six showers between them. 'How different, how very different from the home life of our own dear Queen', as the anonymous matron said. Charles was hardly living the generally accepted idea of a royal prince's cosseted existence.

The coldness between Charles and myself persisted, if it didn't actually intensify. I was in the doghouse as far as he was concerned – metaphorically and literally. I had two-roomed flat, sharing the bathroom and kitchen with two members of the teaching staff who had accommodation similar to mine. These quarters, next to the main house where the boys lived, were the former dog kennels!

Charles was still brooding over Don Green's departure. He continued to be distant and uncommunicative with me, limiting his conversation to the bare essentials for me to do my job. Yet there was more to his surliness than the loss of his friend: there was his loss of rank in Gordonstoun's complicated promotion system for the pupils.

The system totally baffled me, and, I suspect, some of the pupils themselves. The various 'ranks' were: School Uniform, Junior Training Plan, Senior Training Plan, White Stripe, Colour Bearer Candidate, Colour Bearer (prefect, elected by fellow pupils) Helper (head of house, appointed by the housemaster) and Guardian (head boy, appointed by the headmaster). Charles had progressed to the Junior Training Plan, where the boys kept a record of their own 'lates' and other misdemeanours, and imposed their own punishments in a strict honour system. It was an entirely personal and private record not studied by staff or other boys: a sort of silent confessional. As a punishment for his involvement in the cherry brandy incident – really an act of simple naïvety with no mischievous intent – the Prince was taken off the plan. In a manner of speaking he had been reduced to the ranks, and that deepened the dark depression that seemed to be his permanent mood. There was some justification for his feelings, but that didn't make him any the easier to get on with.

Earlier, when Chief Superintendent Perkins told me that I had been appointed as Charles's detective, he said that in future officers would take it in turns to do the duty to avoid any possibility of Charles's again becoming too attached to any one policeman. At this point I was almost glad that my tour of duty with him was going to be only three months. Well, if Prince Charles could stick it out, I told myself, so could I, although three months of boredom loomed on the horizon like a big, black cloud.

The turning-point in our relationship was totally unexpected and dramatically revelatory. I was sitting watching television as usual one evening when there was a quiet knock at the door. It was Prince Charles.

'I was just wondering whether I could have a look at your television,' he said diffidently. It was a tone I had not heard him use before.

'Of course,' I replied, trying not to sound elated. I drew up a chair for him and passed him a cup of coffee.

We sat watching the box for a while without speaking. I was delighted that he had made this first move, but I was determined not to rush things. Then, after a while, he put a question to me that was heartbreaking in its implications. It took me completely off balance; at the same time it gave me an insight into the young Prince's character and his lifestyle that totally changed my view of him.

'Do you ever get lonely?' he asked.

'Most people get lonely, once in a while,' I replied.

He was silent for some moments then said, 'But what about you? Do you get lonely?'

'Oh, yes. Often.'

The answer seemed to satisfy him. After all, in asking the question he had made himself quite vulnerable.

Any resentment I might have felt about his previous attitude towards me was swept away forever. I became aware of a side of his character that hadn't occurred to me before. I realized that in some respects he was an underprivileged youth. At Gordonstoun, Cheam School before then, and Cambridge afterwards he said that it was difficult for him to make friends because he couldn't be sure who were the ones who genuinely liked him and who were the ones who were 'trying to suck up' to him because of his position. 'It's the wrong ones who make the approaches,' he said. Well, at least he couldn't put me in that category: I hadn't made any approach.

After that first night Charles came to my room most evenings to watch the news on television and to collect his post. Gradually he opened up, and although we were half a generation and a whole social world apart, a relationship of genuine friendship gradually developed between us. In all diffidence, it was based on trust, for Charles was incapable of deception or dishonesty, and I was determined to be always equally as straightforward with him. Saying that he was always strictly honest may make him sound priggish or too good to be true, but he never gave that impression; after all, that was his upbringing. It was easy to see that he was aware of his responsibilities from an early age – understandably so, for being brought up in a palace and seeing how one's parents are treated by everyone are pretty forceful lessons!

Nor, I hope, do I sound holier-than-thou. The young Charles was not the sort of person you could easily lie to even if you wanted to. At its very lowest, it was simply that I had no axe to grind by being dishonest, and I wanted to earn the respect of the future king. Honesty was the best way to serve him.

Charles's frequent evening visits to watch television became a feature of our relationship. He turned to me for advice about some of his problems, which I did my best to give. One evening he came and told me that he'd been getting so much unsolicited advice from so many people on every conceivable subject, all different, that he didn't know which advice to take. (I assumed he did not include my advice in this category!) Among the various matters that worried him were whose invitations to accept and how to decline the other invitations gracefully and diplomatically, which boys would make good friends, and which would be best to keep away from. All I could say was that in the end he was the only one who could decide what was the right thing for him to do. His best – his only – sensible course was to listen to what everyone had to say, weigh it all up and then make up his own mind. At first I was surprised that he had asked for my advice, but later I realized that someone in Prince Charles's position is always surrounded by people wanting to press their counsel on him. So I took care not to offer gratuitous advice on anything outside my own sphere of security and to give it only when asked.

He remained angry at what he considered to be the unfair treatment of Don Green. He never forgave the woman journalist concerned, although she was only doing her job as anyone else in her place would have done it. He could not even bring himself to speak her name, always referring to her darkly as 'that woman....'

From quite an early age he had to learn to live with the sharp thorn in his flesh of criticism in the press, which was doubly galling to him because he could never reply to it. He was an obvious target for ill-informed and often totally fictitious stories. People with narrow, minority opinions, and near-nonentities who wanted to get their names in the paper could count on coverage by expressing some moral indignation about the Prince's behaviour. Privately he was surprised and puzzled by attack on him by a Free Church minister who sternly disapproved of his going skiing on a Sunday. There was an occasion when the Lord's Day Observance Society thundered on about 'desecration of the Sabbath' when Princess Margaret bought Charles and Anne an ice-cream on a Sunday. Less unreasonably, the League Against Cruel Sports condemned him for shooting stags. They'd already had a go at him for shooting pheasant at Sandringham with his cousin Norton Knatchbull. But whatever the case against hunting of all kinds, any criticism of Charles really should be aimed at his family for bringing him up to take part in blood 'sports' in his impressionable years. Every king since Edward VII has shot birds and beasts with every sign of enthusiasm and pleasure.

Charles's attitude towards the press must have been further coloured by his father's attitude towards the vast majority of journalists, which was markedly abrasive. Although Charles's own relations with the media have mellowed in recent years, in his youth he had his father's dislike, or worse, of the press.

One of the rules at Gordonstoun was that no unofficial photographs were to be taken of Charles. It was a rule that was easily observed because press photographers could be kept at arm's length in the school grounds. However, there was an occasion when a visitor to the school, a German student named Jurgen von Jordan, was wandering around firing off his camera right, left and centre. I tackled him about this and he told me that he had the headmaster's permission.

'But not to take photographs of Prince Charles,' I told him. 'It's Mr Chew's rule that photographs of him are forbidden.'

'I haven't taken any photographs of Prince Charles,' he assured me, but I wasn't satisfied. I demanded the film from his camera and told him that I would send it to Scotland Yard for developing and printing. The photographs would be returned to him – free of charge! – but any pictures of the Prince would be confiscated. Von Jordan again assured me that he hadn't taken any pictures of Charles.

I sent the film with a covering letter to Chief Superintendent Perkins. In due course the developed photographs came back with a note from Perkins to the effect that all the pictures were quite harmless, with none of Charles.

I opened the packet.

The first four photographs were of Charles, on his own. Maybe Chief Superintendent Perkins didn't recognize him.

While Charles was still a Gordonstoun student he had a rather more dramatic and amusing brush with professional photographers. In September 1964 he and Anne went to Athens for the wedding of King Constantine of the Hellenes and Princess Anne-Marie of Denmark. Charles was one of a dozen young men who took it in turns to hold crowns over the heads of the bride and groom.

After the ceremony Charles and Anne went sunbathing with the Swedish Crown Prince Gustaf and some German cousins at Vouliagmeni, near Athens. Greek naval police protected the royal party, but three determined French press photographers managed to get through this mini-blockade on a raft.

There was something of a skirmish which ended with the photographers going for an impromptu fullyclothed swim. The French press was outraged, totally ignoring the photographers' intrusion on the party's privacy. Charles was saddled with the blame – or credit – for the ducking.

I went to London Airport to meet Charles and Anne and accompany them on their flight to Aberdeen. Charles was returning to Gordonstoun, while Anne was going to Balmoral. On the journey north they chatted about the great time they'd had in Greece – apart from unwelcome press attention. They still chuckled about ducking the photo-graphers with all their equipment, perhaps the first time they'd got their own back on troublesome pressmen. In fact, from what I could gather later it seemed that the German cousins were responsible, but Charles didn't seem to worry in the least that he was generally thought to be the moving spirit.

Recently someone has written of Charles's time at Gordonstoun that it left a deep impression on him, one that has been reflected time and again in later life. Gordonstoun may have been the ideal school for the physical, extrovert Prince Philip. For the shyer, basically private, less physical and more artistically inclined Charles it required a far greater effort to come to terms with its demands. I had the strong impression that he did his best at the school less for himself than to please his father, and to live up to his standards.

It had been made clear to the school by Charles's parents that he was not to be given any special treatment because of his rank. The trouble was, he was special, and there could be no disguising it. Name tapes for his clothes were 'won' by souvenir hunters from his spool in the linen room. In the same way socks and underpants mysteriously disappeared from the laundry and a book of poetry with his name on vanished. Some masters did give him special treatment, but it was of a negative kind: he was subjected to a sort of inverted snobbery. One master frequently called him 'Windsor' and 'Charlie boy'. His housemaster, Bob Whitby, was well known for the way he shouted at the younger boys. With one thing and another, it was no wonder that Charles was far from happy at the beginning of his time at Gordonstoun. In fact, he pleaded with his grandmother, the Queen Mother, to intercede with his parents to have him taken away from the 'gruesome' school. She gently refused to interfere.

So, there could be no getting away from the fact that Charles was different from all the other boys there. The cherry brandy incident brought home to him that he had to do all he could not to attract attention to himself. He couldn't risk taking part in the mild rule-breaking of some of his fellow-pupils, like going to an out-of-bounds café and rather obviously chatting up the girls.

Bob Whitby has subsequently said that he was aware that Charles was unhappy during his first two years at Gordonstoun, but he had seen many boys unhappy for their first two years. Had Charles been unhappy in his third year, then Whitby would have begun to worry, he said. I thought this was very hard on Charles at the time, and I still do. I cannot believe that a lifestyle which makes a youth unhappy for a couple of years is altogether good for him. Because I was not a member of the staff, and because Charles learned that I was to be trusted, he allowed his defences to drop when we were alone, and I could see how very miserable he often was. The fact that he overcame the periods of depression he suffered is a testimony more to his strength of character than to the system.

For the most part Charles kept his feelings to himself in the presence of his fellow-pupils and masters. He hid the unhappiness caused by some of the treatment he received. He bore the physical victimization stoically, but the loneliness and forced awareness of his difference from the other boys were harder to bear. The problem was aggravated by the fact that it was difficult for him to make friends – although, as I have said, he made some – at Gordonstoun as it was during all his scholastic life, earlier at Cheam and later at Cambridge. Worthwhile potential friends hung back for fear of being thought sycophantic. At Gordonstoun the boys were quite savage with anyone they thought was 'crawling' to Charles. Prince Alexander of Yugoslavia was told to show Charles round the place on his first day, and was cruelly nicknamed 'Sponge' by the other boys as a result. It took Alexander quite a while to live it down. The effect on Charles himself can easily be imagined.

It may seem fanciful now, but at the time there were occasions when the boy's solitary courage irresistibly reminded me of an incident in the life of his grandfather, King George VI. He was a basically quiet, private man with a hesitant stammer which must have been acutely embarrassing for one so much in the public eye and so often required to make speeches. At the opening of the Festival of Britain in 1951 George VI stood alone on the steps of St Paul's Cathedral, with newsreel cameras from all over the world focused on him and the microphones of a dozen countries' broadcasting systems ready to pick up and transmit his every word...and hesitation. Not until some years later was I old enough to appreciate what enormous moral courage he summoned up to face an ordeal that must have been agonizing for him. In a lesser degree Charles showed that same duty-inspired inner courage.

Not long ago I read somewhere that Queen Elizabeth the Queen Mother has said that Charles reminded her of her husband, George VI, more than any of her other grandchildren. Maybe I wasn't being too fanciful after all.

So the lonely young Charles kept his emotions tightly within himself. It was perhaps only with me that – consciously or unconsciously – he allowed glimpses of his true feelings to show. I could never imagine him asking one of the other boys 'Do you ever get lonely?', or, for that matter, one of the masters. I suppose that to him I was a sort of neutral observer. We came from totally different worlds: I wasn't a member of the social class of the boys there, nor of the intellectual class of the teachers. I was a representative of the Common Man, of all the future King Charles III's subjects. Perhaps most importantly, my first – indeed my only – loyalty was to Charles himself.

In any case, I believe that from that memorable evening onwards I came to know Charles better than any man alive during his formative years at Gordonstoun and Cambridge.

We spoke about many things during the following years. And yet I can never remember his mentioning his father to me, either at Gordonstoun or at Cambridge. Of all the boys and young men I spoke to at length he was the only one whom I cannot remember ever talking about his father. Not ever. It took some time for this to dawn on me, and when it did, I was quite taken aback. Perhaps it was simply reluctance to talk about close family affairs, although he occasionally mentioned his mother, usually with reference to her official duties. Other boys had no such inhibitions to talking about their fathers with me, but then none of them was heir to the throne. Inevitably I was curious about this omission from Charles's conversation, although, of course, I never took the initiative in raising personal matters. Nevertheless, I could not help but wonder whether Charles's silence was more significant than any long conversations on the subject.

4 Friends and Neighbours

Although Charles had a rough time of it in his early years, they were not times of unrelieved misery and solitude.

He made a few friends, but none of them became really close. Already at Gordonstoun when Charles arrived was a German cousin, Prince Guelf, the fifteen-year-old son of Prince Philip's sister Princess Sophie of Hanover, but any friendship between Charles and Guelf never progressed very far. It has also been said that Norton Knatchbull was one of his friends because he was a grandson of Charles's own beloved great-uncle, Lord Mountbatten, and because the boys had met before Gordonstoun. However, they had been barely more than acquaintances. They were both in Windmill Lodge, but Norton Knatchbull was a year ahead of Charles, which in some ways was a greater gulf than mere geographical separation. They became closer friends later in life.

One good friend, within the limits of which Charles seemed capable at the time, was Philip Bagnall, who came from East Africa and spoke Swahili. Geordie Gordon, a nephew of the Marquess of Huntly, was one of Charles's less intimate friends. (George Gordon, the first Marquess of Huntly, built the original Gordonstoun House, of course.)

Compared with my own standard education, the emphasis on practical learning at Gordonstoun was a revelation to me. The boys frequently went out on expeditions. Robert Birley, the history master there, took the boys on field trips and, of course, I went along with Charles. His interest in archaeology and anthropology, which he was to read at Cambridge, was aroused at Gordonstoun.

Normally I kept well in the background and had come to be taken as a sort of piece of moving scenery. On one occasion, however, I thought I'd lend a hand with the lesson...

Birley took the boys to caves by the beach at Covesea, between Lossiemouth and Hopeman. They crawled into one small cave on all fours, trying to visualize how primitive man used to live. The roof of the cave was so low that it was impossible to stand up straight.

The scene was most effective, with a flickering wood fire casting large, dancing shadows on the narrow walls and roof as we sat in the cave. Birley told the class that at the time of the original cave-dwellers the atmosphere would have been smoky because the wood for the fire would have come from the beach, washed up by the tide. On an impulse I threw on to the fire a sack I had been sitting on which had become quite damp from the sand.

It made the place smoky, all right – much smokier than primitive man would have suffered, otherwise he wouldn't have survived. The dense, acrid smoke was bad enough, but it brought down what seemed to be thousands of spiders. I glanced at Charles. He was suffering agonies of horror at the spiders and, I think, embarrassment to think that his normally very correctly behaved (at least, I tried to be) personal shadow could have done something quite so stupid.

Through all the coughing and spluttering, at last came the calm tones of Robin Birley.

'I know I was looking for realism, but this is ridiculous.' Then he paused, looked towards me and made a mock menacing gesture. 'You're not going to let him get away with that, are you?' he asked the boys.

They started moving towards me, muttering all sorts of horrible threats. I slipped out of the cave, closely chased along the beach by a dozen half-angry, half-amused youths. I didn't want to be thrown into the cold sea, so I beat a retreat, without a great deal of dignity, I'm afraid. As I ran for it, I thought it was just as well that no outsider could see Prince Charles's gallant bodyguard, meant to protect him from all perils, being put to flight by a gang of schoolboys.

The boys were allowed to wander around the countryside and down to the sea when they weren't occupied with their demanding timetable. Charles enjoyed country walks either on his own or with any visitors that came to see him, rather than taking them on a tour of the school. He also accepted a very occasional invitation to take part in a shoot or to have Sunday lunch with the Lord-Lieutenant of Morayshire, Captain Tennant, or the Vice-Lieutenant. It seemed to me that he was happier in the company of people older than himself – a result, perhaps, of being brought up in his pre-school days mainly away from other children. And, of course, with older people of some standing there could be no question of any 'sucking up' to him. At least, not much.

There was an incident years later at Cambridge, when he was on one of his archaeological digs with other 'ark and ant' – archaeology and anthropology – students. When the group unwittingly wandered onto private land the owner popped up unexpectedly and started to castigate them vigorously...until he saw Prince Charles. Instantly the landowner's attitude did a 180-degree turn: he practically started wringing his cap in his hands and became effusive. Charles was horribly embarrassed and much more uncomfortable than when he was being shouted at. He turned pillar-box red and hurried off.

My overwhelming impression was that there was a paradox in the young Charles's nature. He was keenly aware of being lonely, and he was glad when he gradually came to make friends, at a certain level. Yet he seemed happiest in his own company. His favourite relaxation was fishing, which is as lonely a pursuit as anyone can have.

He was able to indulge his passion for fishing when he visited the Queen Mother at Birkhall, her home on the Balmoral estate. It was built during the Jacobite Rising of 1715 by Charles Gordon and purchased in 1852 for the then Prince of Wales, later Edward VII. It is not as large as Balmoral Castle, and has been considered too small for a royal residence on a number of occasions but is now the Deeside home of the Queen Mother. She was a very keen on fly fishing herself and was quite expert.

It was on a visit to Birkhall with Charles and a couple of his friends that I first spoke to the Queen Mother at any length, and I shall always remember her as being the one member of the royal family who really showed me any consideration. I had driven over from Gordonstoun with Prince Charles and was surprised to find the Queen Mother waist-deep in the icy water with her gillie Mr Pearl beside her. She waded out of the river to greet her grandson, and it was clear that they were very fond of each other. (Another example of how Charles was more at ease with people older than himself.) Then the Queen Mother turned to me and explained the layout of the house and grounds, which I needed to know in my capacity as the Prince's protection officer.

I'm afraid that I repaid the Queen Mother's thoughtfulness very badly. On a subsequent occasion, after he had taken his O-levels, Charles went on a trip to Balmoral with a couple of friends. From there they went on to the River Esk. He spent hour after hour waist-deep in the water and was still fishing at 2 a.m. I thought there must be something in this fishing business to fascinate Charles so much and that I'd try my hand at fishing myself. All I managed to hook was a tree, and in trying to free the line from it I broke one of the Queen Mother's rods and tore my suit.

However, there was a much darker side to this expedition which came close to costing Charles his life.

Soon after the ice was broken by Charles's coming into my room to watch television the question of my authority – or lack of it – arose. It had not come up until then because there had been practically no communication between us anyway.

The incident that provoked it was relatively unimportant. After the Prince and the other members of the Gordonstoun orchestra had played at a concert at Elgin town hall the boys got ready to board the coach that would take them back to the school. As usual, I had a quick look outside to make sure there was nothing to worry about. However, there was a larger-than-usual platoon of press photographers and journalists waiting to snatch pictures and get quotes from Charles when he came out. Normally between us we could manage to outflank them, but on this occasion there was no way of doing it, as we had to go from the town hall door across the pavement to the door of the coach, and I feared that there might be a number of local rowdies among the usual peaceable members of the public.

I hurried back into the hall and told Charles not to go out with the others but to hang on with one of the masters until I gave him the word to get into the coach. He looked as if he was on the point of rebelling, or at least arguing with me about it, but he stayed put.

The whole group of us, jammed together in a minor jostling scrum with me in the middle, piled out of the hall and into the coach. The fact that I was with the group persuaded the photographers that Charles was with us. They pressed forward but, with all the boys dressed exactly the same and much about the same size, they couldn't make out one boy from another. Without meaning to the photographers did us a good turn by forming a barrier between us and the general public, including any potentially annoying rowdies. The boys were enjoying themselves enormously.

A journalist asked one of the boys at the back of the group 'Which one is Prince Charles?' which struck me as showing a marvellous lack of awareness. Still, as I said, all the boys were much of a size and were all wearing the same clothes, so perhaps he could be excused.

By now Charles was quite popular with most of his schoolfellows, and they were pleased to help him – and do the press in the eye at the same time. The boy replied immediately with total aplomb, 'He's already on the coach.'

The journalists and curious moved away from the door and along both sides of the coach, trying to see in the windows, which were above head-height of someone on the ground. At that moment I nipped back to the hall and signalled to Charles and the teacher. They hurried onto the coach without being noticed. The door slammed shut behind us and we were off.

This dodge of smuggling Charles aboard a coach in the middle of a milling group became a favourite trick of the boys.

The next night, I think it was, Charles and I discussed the Elgin town hall incident and the subject of my actually telling him to stay put. I said that I should never ask – tell – him to do anything I didn't consider to be absolutely necessary for his own safety or dignity. However, when I did ask him to do something, I expected him to do it right there and then, without question. If he couldn't see why I told him to do whatever it was, I'd be glad to give a full explanation...later.

I think that rather took him aback for a moment; and to be honest, I was a little taken aback myself by my own temerity, albeit that I was talking to a thirteen-year-old. Much later I realized that, in spite of his shyness, Charles had a natural authority about him even at that early age. He was aware of his position without being big-headed about it; he had a sense of duty beyond his youth.

There must have been times when having to do the things I asked – or told – him to do must have seemed irksome or pointless. If there were such times, the memory of a certain journey to Scotland would soon have changed his mind.

Someone once wrote that 'Nobody....believes that Charles is in the slightest danger; but the infinitesimal chance of the incalculable lunatic cannot be quite left out of account....' The one person who could never afford to leave it quite out of account was myself. It took a constant self-reminding and conscious effort of will not to forget it. There were occasions, though, when the possibility of that one infinitesimal chance was right in the forefront of my mind, and none more so than on a return journey to Gordonstoun from London.

Charles had been at Buckingham Palace for his birthday and we were returning on the overnight train from Euston Station. When booking a sleeping-compartment Charles always used an alias: sometimes a slightly comic one, sometimes the name of a friend. On this occasion I think he used 'Steven Caldicott'. The idea was to stop anyone noticing his name on the reservations list and tipping off the Press. Of course the train crew and sleeping car attendant recognized Charles as soon as he appeared, but by then he was safely aboard the train.

On this particular journey there was an unusual and unexpected minor commotion in the corridor of the coach. Voices were raised, and there was the tinny sound of the sleeping car attendant's small portable radio.

Charles poked his head out of his compartment and asked me 'Is anything wrong?'

I had to tell him that we had just heard on the radio that President Kennedy had been assassinated. It was, of course, the evening of 22 November 1963.

Charles looked back at me without expression, and after a moment said simply 'Oh.' Then he went back inside his compartment. I was absolutely certain that we were both thinking the same thing: that many people are murdered, but only presidents, kings and princes are assassinated. Charles himself was one of that small, exalted group of those who possess power or rank that make them potential targets of a madman.

I slept even more uneasily than usual on that journey.

On only one occasion did Charles seriously question my decision, and then only obliquely. I had been with him some years when he went to the Cumberland Hotel by London's Marble Arch to attend a farewell dinner in honour of his former housemaster at Gordonstoun, Bob Whitby, in October 1968. We arrived a little early, so I told the chauffeur to drive round the block. Earlier the Prince had commented on the presence of a small crowd outside Buckingham Palace when we left, saying something like, 'I don't understand how all these people know when I'm attending a purely private function.' As we passed the Cumberland Hotel entrance a second time Charles noticed that another small crowd were waiting there, presumably in the hope of seeing him and giving him a cheer. Indirectly, but quite clearly, he let me know that he suspected me of leaking the information.

I told him outright that I hadn't, and I shouldn't dream of doing it, for two reasons: first, not to jeopardize his safety and comfort; and second, not to risk my job as his protection officer. I pointed out that being stared at and cheered by crowds of people was an occupational hazard for someone of his position: it was going to be a permanent part of his life. He took my other point that the time to start worrying was when there was no cheering crowd, or when a sullen one just stared in silence.

Years later at Cardiff I was to remember vividly my own words.

Whatever other help it may have been to Charles to come and talk to me privately after school hours, at least I was able to encourage him to stand up to some of the other boys, who picked on him for a number of reasons. He was a relatively new boy, and a rather podgy, withdrawn one at that, at least to begin with. In fact he was the archetypal victim of boarding-school nasties, even though Gordonstoun would not like to admit that they had any at their school. Most of all, of course, he was Prince Charles. Tormenting him obviously appealed to a cruel streak in some twisted minds, and there was the added perverted pleasure of persecuting the heir to the throne. It was a cheap and easy way for certain pupils to assert what they thought was their own superiority.

One evening Charles was looking particularly gloomy and I asked him what was wrong. At first he was reluctant to say anything, but when I pressed him he admitted to me that some of the boys were getting at him. There was no hint of an appeal for sympathy in his tone, but I felt he was seeking advice.

I told him much of what I have just said, but he was already aware of this. He knew why he was being picked on; what he didn't know was what to do about it. I went on to explain that he simply had to stand up to the bullies. He hesitated.

'Look,' I said, 'I know you're not afraid. I've seen you playing rugby and taking some hard knocks without flinching.'

But that wasn't what was bothering him. It was that Charles was aware that any story of him fighting – even a bully – would reflect badly on his family. Perhaps the cherry brandy incident had really brought home to him how ready the press were to seize on any incident that concerned him and magnify it. And I knew that he felt keenly the remarks that had been made about his hunting and his shooting on a Sunday. So, in his everyday life he always had to tread Agag-like while other boys could romp about cheerfully and heavy-footed, unconcerned about public comment. Charles also worried about being thought big-headed and stuck-up because of his rank, although he was far from self-important. Then there was the royal family custom of never answering back to hostile comment from the press and elsewhere, however baseless. He had been brought up in the tradition of biting your tongue in the face of unfair criticism. That may be all right for the adults in the more or less insulated royal family in the great big world outside, but it was a recipe for misery in the closed society of a boarding school.

So, I told him forcibly that here he had to fight back – not necessarily with his fists – and to stand up to bullying. Then, in what I thought was a moment of inspiration, I said he owed to his own and his family's honour not to back down in the face of schoolboy persecution.

It seemed to work. He gradually appeared less depressed and subject to tormenting by other boys.

Eventually some of the other boys realized that Charles's having a reliable confidant could be a great help. From time to time boys came to my flat to chat and ask for my advice on rather different problems. If they had gone to a master with them, the information would be passed on to their parents, which was the last thing the boys wanted. They knew that their confidences stopped at my door.

Sometimes I found that what a few of them had to say was as sad, in its way, as Charles's 'Do you ever get lonely?'. Although the boys were in their teens – some of them very early teens – they were experienced enough to understand that they had been sent to boarding-school to get them out of the way: they weren't really wanted at home. Then Daddy could entertain Aunt Laura and Mummy could entertain Uncle Julian. In addition, the parents could always justify things by saying, 'Well, my son went to Gordonstoun, you know – he was there with Prince Charles, as a matter of fact.' Children can often be perceptive beyond their years.

Charles's way of life in school, and later at college, was totally different from his life outside. It's true that at Cambridge he wouldn't have to make his own bed or clean his rooms; it's equally true he did some light cooking for himself and friends, but on his weekends away from Gordonstoun or Cambridge, either at a royal residence or at friends' estates, there were armies of servants to do the unpleasant chores. In his first formative years he was brought up in an environment distanced from the world of cleaning-materials, polish and washing-powder. For all his fairly spartan upbringing at Gordonstoun, where he finally came into contact with them all, at Cambridge Charles sometimes found it difficult to reconcile himself to the

transition from weekend cosseted luxury to a weekday
do-it-yourself comfort.

At Gordonstoun he'd already had some practice – not
always successful – at trying to avoid unpleasant jobs. I often
wondered whether Charles's Junior Training Plan included a
note about one – at least – of his sly dodges when he was sent
on a punishment run round the South Lawn because his
locker wasn't tidy enough when it was inspected. (There
were a number of standard punishments for errant pupils as
well as being sent on runs: cleaning sports equipment,
kitchen duty and humping dustbins, for example. Charles
seemed to have more than his fair share of dustbin duties:
further examples of negative discrimination, I suppose.)

To return to this punishment run. Apparently Charles was
soon bored with the walk, jog, walk, jog of the run. I found
out that he sloped into the bushes for a breather and joined
the jogging group after a couple of laps. Maybe some people
would call it cheating. I prefer to think of it as an
opportunistic exercise of initiative.

There were odd occasions when he would Try It On with
me. He would come into my room with his muddy
shooting-boots and put them down 'casually'. Then a little
later:

'Hmm, I'll be needing my boots next week.'

I would say nothing, and nor would Charles.

A day or two after that: 'We mustn't forget my boots. I'll
be taking them with me next week.'

Finally: 'I'll be needing my boots this weekend.'

To which I replied firmly: 'Then you'd better clean them.'

Charles accepted it in good part, giving his famous
semi-apologetic grin. He picked up his boots and took them
off to clean. He'd think up some new ruse to lumber me with
the chore the next time.

In retrospect I suppose that this demonstrated that the
starch was going out of our relationship.

One of Charles's pet dislikes was having his hair cut, and I
was often cast in the role of the RSM at an Officer Cadet
Training Unit, having to say 'Get your hair cut ....sir !' A
local hairdresser named Barry used to visit the school.
Charles seemed to look forward to his visits as enthusi-
astically as if he were Sweeney Todd, but, with me urging

him on, he used to have a light trim every time Barry came to the school. Sometimes it was hardly anything more than a token snip or two. However, it meant that Charles could honestly say that he'd had his hair cut at Barry's last visit whenever he was asked by his housemaster, Bob Whitby, who was a stickler for all the boys being neat and tidy.

When a photograph appeared in the press of Charles with a fringe it was suggested that he wanted to look like one of the Beatles. In fact it was nothing of the kind. It was simply that he was reluctant to appear like a squaddy or a convict, and his longish hair had been blown about a little at the airport. Whatever he may have thought of the Beatles, one thing is certain: he was always conscious of his public image as heir to the throne. His only escape from the straitjacket of his position would be in his stage performances.

5 The Play's the Thing – and a High Temperature

When I first joined Charles at Gordonstoun he was not a particularly athletic youth. He took part in the organized games and activities because he had to, not because he was naturally an enthusiastic sportsman. But as the years passed, he became a much more physically active man. Whatever else Gordonstoun did for him, it was successful in developing his physical side.

Cricket is a fairly harmless game; at least, it was then, and it didn't cause me any concern when he played. In any case, Charles had no great talent for the game – or even a small one, to be honest – so he was only a lukewarm cricketer. It was not in his character to stand about in a cricket field doing almost nothing for half a day. (Although as far as I could see, that's what he did when he went fishing.) During the time I was with him his best performance, I suppose, was at a country house match against a team of Grand Prix drivers at the home of the Brabourne family. He scored 20 before the late Graham Hill had him caught by Bruce McLaren. (Lord Brabourne is married to Countess Mountbatten of Burma, the late Lord Mountbatten's daughter, and their eldest son, now Lord Romsey, was formerly Norton Knatchbull, Charles's friend at Gordonstoun.)

When it came to rugby Charles must have known what he was in for. In later life boys would be able to dine out on their stories of when they sent the future king sprawling in the mud. So everyone wanted to tackle the heir to the throne and dump him heavily. Prince Charles took two or three tackles to most people's one. I was sure that in the general excitement he was even tackled by some of his own team.

I was constantly concerned about his safety: not his life, but his health. A broken limb was always a possibility, if not a probability. Nevertheless, Charles, not naturally a macho boy, didn't flinch. It was a display of quiet, cold courage. Although I had no real right to do so, I felt proud of him. Later it came to me that my feelings were a sign of the way our relationship was developing.

When Charles broke his nose – or, more accurately, when someone broke it for him – the line had to be drawn against his continued participation in rugby matches. I insisted that he give up rugby just after I had learned about a Royal Marine Commando technique for killing an enemy by driving the nose bone up into the brain. So that was that: no more rugby.

It was no great sacrifice for him. Charles ruefully admitted to me one evening that he was always picked for lock forward, the second row of the scrum – perhaps the least enviable position to play. He never moaned about it publicly, though.

He also played soccer, with more vigour and application than skill, despite being captain of football at Cheam School before coming to Gordonstoun. On the evidence of what what I saw there was cause for strong suspicion that his rank rather than his footballing ability got him his captaincy at Cheam. Certainly that season, under his captaincy, the First XI lost every game! He played some golf at Lossiemouth, but soon lost interest in it.

Charles was quite good at tennis, though, and we played a lot together on the Gordonstoun courts, which were near Windmill Lodge. I usually managed to win because I had been coached by Jaroslav Drobny, a former Wimbledon champion. Charles's coach was Dan Maskell.

From an early age Prince Charles grew to love sailing, even though his first experience of it, at Cowes in his father's boat *Bluebottle*, made him sea-sick, he admitted to me once. At the time he was only nine years old, and a bad start like that might well have put off a less determined boy, or one who didn't have as forceful a father as Charles. Yet Charles quite soon developed an ambition for a naval career, like his father and Lord Mountbatten, 'Uncle Dickie'.

He first wore naval uniform in November 1963, when he was fifteen years old. While Charles was still at Gordonstoun he went to HMS *Vernon*, a shore-based naval establishment at Portsmouth, for a week's training course with other cadets from the school.

He seemed to enjoy the experience for a number of reasons. First, of course, was that this was a first rung on the ladder of a naval career. Then there was the presence of a fellow fan of the Goons: Petty Officer R. Joce, the medical orderly.

A more positive and subjective incentive to go sailing, however, was that it got him away from the press. But not always. When the boys went rowing or sailing in the harbour it was naval policy for them to be accompanied by safety boat, with the medical petty officer in the crew. As he was in the boat, I was invited to go with him if I wanted to.

From a purely selfish point of view the idea of a boat trip or two was attractive enough for me to accept, but in any case I felt I should go along as a matter of duty, to see what Charles was doing. Some perceptive reporter obviously saw me and his paper published a story to the effect that Prince Charles's parents wanted him to have the life of a normal schoolboy, so did this mean that every boy was accompanied by a gun-toting detective? It was another irritating example of a fabricated story of half-truths which could not be countered. The safety boat had to be there anyway, and I certainly didn't carry a gun. It wasn't enough totally to spoil Charles's week, though.

In 1967, while Charles was still waiting for his examination results to come through we went to Cowes. Although only 19, he was now quite accomplished at sailing small yachts as far as I could see and from comments that others made about his abilities. He raced there for the first time in a borrowed boat, a Flying Fifteen named *Labrador*. His father took part in the same race in a boat called *Cowslip*.

Charles enjoyed the advantage of having Uffa Fox, the celebrated yacht-designer and sailor, as his crew. It was rather like having Ari Vatenen as his co-driver in an amateur motor rally. Although the tiller broke just before the start, which delayed their departure, *Labrador*, with me cheering it on (silently: vulgar shouting was hardly the thing for the purlieus of the Royal Yacht Squadron) gradually started overhauling the other yachts. There was no question of Charles's winning the race, there was too much to make up in the time that was left, but he made up nine places to finish thirteenth.

Prince Philip, in *Cowslip*, finished twenty-second and last.

On the surface it was a small thing, Charles (and Uffa Fox) beating his father, but I was delighted for him. Even after the years at Gordonstoun and the two terms he'd spent at Timbertop the Prince was still somewhat conscious of his father's achievements and his expectations. Playing the lead in *Macbeth*, while Philip could get only a minor role when he was at Gordonstoun, was a small victory of a kind. However, acting was an activity that really didn't interest Philip all that much; yachting was an entirely different matter. It was a manly, outdoor activity that appealed to the extrovert, physical-rather-than-intellectual Duke. And Charles had beaten him at it, fair and square.

Maybe I am reading too much into the brief moments in which I saw of the son and father after the race, but it seemed to me that Philip was trying to conceal that he was, in a manner of speaking, quite miffed, while Charles was equally trying to conceal that he was quite chuffed.

There was one sport Charles undoubtedly delighted in, and that was skiing: he went on regular skiing holidays in various parts of Europe when he was still a schoolboy. I can recall three skiing holidays he went on while he was at Gordonstoun: once to Switzerland as the guest of Prince Ludwig of Hesse and twice to Liechtenstein. It was a sport entirely suited to his character. It is exhilarating and has a thrilling element of danger that appealed to a masculine – without being macho – trait that was developing in him. Skiing can also be challenging without needing to be competitive, so Prince Charles would not have to prove himself like a leader of a tribe by beating all the other members of his group; as far as he was concerned it was not a pressure sport. And, of course, it can be a solitary sport practised in very open country. Charles was often happiest on long solitary walks away from everyone.

However, the sport must have lost some of its appeal for

him since his friend Major Hugh Lindsay was killed by an avalanche in the Alps in 1988. It must have been doubly agonizing for Charles that the tragedy occurred when he was enjoying one of his favourite relaxations.

Philip prodded Charles into taking up polo, and he eventually grew to enjoy this sport for the privileged, too. Good judges said that he became a better rider than his father, but Philip was the better polo player because of his greater competitiveness. In private Charles was undisguisedly delighted when he was awarded a half-blue for representing Cambridge at polo.

Before I arrived at Gordonstoun the Prince had already tried to learn to play the bagpipes and been warned off them because he was such a poor player. I found this difficult to take in, because I never could believe that anyone could play bagpipes well. By the time I got there, he had already started on the trumpet. His first instrument had been provided by Gordonstoun, but he decided he should have an instrument of his own. I accompanied him when he went to buy it in London.

During our walk through Soho to the musical instrument shops we inevitably passed a number of establishments of dubious business. Charles was curious about some of them, and commented that it seemed a strange sort of place for people to come for 'French Lessons'.

Some of the local girls lurking in doorways must have puzzled him as well when they invited him, 'Fancy a good time, sonny? Why don't you bring your father as well?' They weren't referring to His Royal Highness Prince Philip, Duke of Edinburgh, but to me, whom they took to be the young lad's father. At least, that's what I told myself at the time; now I'm not so sure, because I was only nine years older than Charles, and looking after him hadn't aged me that much. Not then, anyway.

Perhaps I was lucky that I am tone deaf and consequently not musically inclined, because Charles's talent as a trumpeter was uncertain, to say the least. Miss Kim Murray, an Elgin music teacher and leader of an orchestra in which Charles played, described him as 'quite brilliant for someone who has been playing only for a short while'. And he played in an ensemble of six instrumentalists who played Handel,

Mozart and Bach at St Luke's and St John's Church at Montrose, and at Elgin town hall. However, I have the distinct impression that Miss Murray's assessment had a strong royalist bias. Charles himself frequently asked members of the audience and fellow-members of the orchestra whether he was playing in tune. Much more significant was the comment that was wrung out of Frau Suzanne Lachmann when Charles played:

'Ach, der trumpet! I cannot stand der trumpet!'

This wonderful German lady originally taught at Kurt Hahn's Salem School and was a refugee from Nazi Germany like Hahn himself. When she came to Britain he helped her get a job.

So, Charles moved on from bagpipes and trumpet to the cello, a change that was inspired by hearing the late Jacqueline du Pré at the Royal Festival Hall during a visit to London. At least the cello wasn't as loud as the trumpet, and in all fairness he had a far better reputation as a cellist than as a trumpeter. Certainly he played in a number of public performances and was not stoned in the streets by music-lovers afterwards.

I think Frau Lachmann gave him his first lessons on the cello at Gordonstoun, and when he went up to Trinity he took lessons from a Mrs McDonald at her home in Brooklands Avenue and a Mrs Hebburn, who lived in Madingley Road, if my memory serves.

Before he went to lessons at these houses I made my usual visit to the premises to size up the entrances and exits and to make a reconnaissance of the streets in the area in case heavy traffic or crowds of any kind meant we had to nip away up a side street. Occasionally I took the chance of an hour off and left Charles alone to have his lesson, and came back later to pick him up. More usually I chatted to – rather than chatted up – the au pair and lent a hand with preparing sandwiches and drinks for the break. Occasionally, too, I came the heavy copper and helped her keep the teacher's children quiet so their racket wouldn't disturb the lesson.

Charles was quite quickwitted about his playing – as he was about most things. I remember that after one recital – at St Giles Cathedral in Edinburgh, I think it was – he said to some of the ladies who had been at the performance, 'While my cello playing may not have been up to scratch at least I managed to blow my own trumpet.' They were delighted with his remark, but they were probably as uncritical of him as was the Elgin music teacher. They would have been equally pleased if he had said something like, 'Pass down the car, please...' As Oscar Wilde said, a wit has only to say 'Pass the salt' to set the table in a roar; an attractive prince has only to say 'What nice weather we're having' to set some ladies in a twitter.

It was clear – at least to those with a more musical ear than mine – that he continued to make progress with the cello when he got to Cambridge. He played in the college orchestra and performed in a concert in Trinity Chapel. I recognized Beethoven's Fifth Symphony – I think – but that was all. The fault was not with the orchestra's playing but with my own severely limited musical appreciation.

Charles was very much an outdoor man, where he could get away from all the pressures of modern living. He found enormous pleasure in solitary walks through the countryside – solitary, that is, except for me, and I took good care to respect his periods of silent reflection when he didn't want to talk. There were times when he seemed totally withdrawn, yet happy and relaxed and complete within himself. Even if I had spoken to him, he probably wouldn't have heard me. Fishing, another of his favourite relaxations, is anything but a gregarious activity, and typical of the sort of thing he enjoyed. I remember once when we were out walking on the Balmoral estate I couldn't help but think 'Make the most of your freedom while you can, because when you're king you won't be able to be alone like this, getting away from all your responsibilities for a moment.'

Another of his great pleasures was acting, which at first sight seems paradoxical but is quite consistent with the other side of his personality. As countless people have pointed out many times, the majority of actors are really introverted; many of them become actors so that, subconsciously, they can conceal their real selves behind the façade of the role they are playing...or they can forget their real selves for a brief moment. (Or because – and this was definitely not the case with Charles – they don't have a personality of their own and need to put one on like make-up and a costume.)

I was told by people who should know that Prince Charles had a genuine talent for acting; at the least he was a good amateur and in any other walk of life, with more time to indulge his hobby, he might have become a first-class one. But, from my close observation of Charles, it was obvious that having a talent for acting was not the only reason he enjoyed it so much. Even when I was with him at Gordonstoun and he was still in his early teens, as I have said, Charles had a strong sense of duty, of what would be demanded of him, whether he liked it or not. From quite a young age he was conscious that a certain standard of behaviour was expected of him, and it was clear to me that he 'would pay the debt I did not owe', the debt that the accident of birth had put on him. In a manner of speaking, in his ordinary daily life he was constantly on stage, but he was playing himself. There was nowhere to hide. Acting in a play was the perfect opportunity to behave in an unprincely fashion without any risk of being accused of irresponsibility. Whenever I watched him in rehearsal or on the stage I was struck by the way the young Prince's natural diffidence, shyness and slight gaucheness all fell away from him. He became assured, authoritative and sure in his movements.

Nor is it any coincidence, I am sure, that his favourite comedians were the Goons; not because he could accurately mimic 'Bluebottle's' voice but because their humour was anarchic and fantastical, as far from his strictly regulated life as can be imagined. Indulging in Goonery was a complete escape, as was walking alone across the moors.

The arrival at Gordonstoun of Eric Anderson (later headmaster at Eton) to teach English opened a door onto a new interest for Charles. He was an extremely pleasant man, and his wife Poppy was no less charming. One of Anderson's tasks was to put on the school plays, and his first production was *Henry V*.

When Anderson joined Gordonstoun there was no school amateur dramatic society as such and so he put a notice on the noticeboard inviting volunteers for the school play. As I glanced at the signatures it was brought home to me once again how different Charles was from all the other pupils at the school. The notice had a list of signatures: Christian names and initials and surnames. And one single Christian name: Charles.

At the auditions it seemed to me that Charles was by far and away the best actor, but I thought that my opinion might be affected by a prejudice stemming from a proprietorial sense of loyalty. In any case, the part of Henry went to another boy. Charles played the Duke of Exeter. Nevertheless, others better qualified than I am agreed with my assessment that he was the best actor in the company; and his failure to get the lead was another example of that inverted snobbery from which Charles suffered (in silence) so much at Gordonstoun, and to some extent later at Cambridge.

Subsequently Anderson admitted that if Charles had been an ordinary boy he would have got the part with no trouble at all. 'But, being a cautious Scot, I gave him the Duke of Exeter. And he did it to the manner born.' Incidentally, this role was played by Prince Philip when he was a pupil at Gordonstoun. There is no doubt that the son's performance was very significantly better than the father's.

I used to hang around backstage while Charles was rehearsing, and some of the boys got me to give a helping hand moving lights and props, but Eric Anderson stopped me doing it. He explained that the boys were there to learn, and if you tried to do too much for them they'd cheerfully let you do it and so would learn nothing themselves. It was a typical Gordonstoun philosophy.

Another show in which Charles appeared, in a minor role of a dragoon guard, was Gilbert and Sullivan's *Patience*. This was produced by Dr McKnight, the school's medical officer, housemaster of Duffus House and teacher of music and English. He also conducted the orchestra. (It seemed that everyone at Gordonstoun was multi-talented.) Dr McKnight also kept me from doing anything backstage.

Henry V was played in the Round Square. It was bitterly cold, and the audience were muffled up in heavy overcoats and rugs. They kept warm with hot soup, with one or two people opting for pocket flasks of whisky. The cold did nothing to cool the audience's enthusiasm, and the play was excellently received.

Charles's performance made it easy for Eric Anderson to

give him the lead in the next school play; indeed it made it inescapable. Anderson chose *Macbeth*, despite the facts that he was a Scot and that the play has the sinister reputation of being unlucky. During rehearsals the young actors worked hard, inspired, I'm sure, by the example of Prince Charles. He was totally professional in attitude towards his acting, as he was always thorough in everything he undertook. He spent a long time studying the character of Macbeth before launching into the play; he was always on time and knew his text.

Someone mentioned that some really superstitious professional actors won't even say the name Macbeth. One or two of the boys entered into the spirit of the thing by calling it, as professionals do, 'the Scottish play'. In fact the production did seem to have a number of unexpected difficulties, and near the end of rehearsals there was a lighting failure just when the Three Witches were due to open the play. It wasn't simply a fuse: the main power lines had been grounded by a fallen tree and half the countryside was blacked out. My own feeling was that the traditional bad luck of *Macbeth* was like the curse of Tutankhamun: quite natural mishaps were blamed on supernatural forces.

In contrast to the alleged dark side of the play, there were a number of lighthearted incidents. During rehearsals Macbeth's crown arrived from the costumiers: it was meant for a real big-head, for it fell down over Charles's eyes. A couple of wags asked if he hadn't got any better crowns at home.

One major problem that had nothing to do with bad luck, natural or supernatural, was that the following January Charles was going to Timbertop School in Australia, so if Gordonstoun was going to have the services of its best actor, the play had to go on before Christmas. This ruled out the possibility of its being presented at the open-air Round Square. The summer nights in Scotland could be pretty nippy; in December there would be a better-than-even chance of snow and ice. It was decided that *Macbeth* would be given at the Georgian-style Services Centre built in 1959-60 to house the watchers (coastguards), fire service and mountain rescue. There was also a changing room for visitors using the adjacent King George V Playing Fields. The upper floor was used as an assembly hall and was spacious enough to take the whole school: ideal for putting on a play. There are stairs which come up into the middle of the assembly hall; the performance was given with two banks of seats on either side of the performing area, an arrangement which I'd never seen before.

Eric Anderson was worried by the fact that the Queen and Prince Philip were coming to see the play. He felt that their presence might put off some of the youthful actors, particularly Charles himself. His concern was pointless. Once again Charles demonstrated one of his sudden, unexpected moments of precocious self-possession. He was backstage with the rest of the cast, putting on costumes and make-up, when the Queen and the Duke started to make their way up the stairs. The audience rose and the school orchestra played the national anthem.

'Oh, dear,' Charles said. 'My mother will be so nervous.'

There were a couple of fraught moments during the play. First, the Three Witches cry, 'All hail, Macbeth, who shall be king hereafter!' That set the hall in a brief buzz. Then, those who knew the play well must have awaited the last scene with a certain excitement, for there is the stage direction '*Enter Macduff with Macbeth's head*'... However, the Queen was spared that.

The Queen was clearly delighted to see her son playing the lead with such talent. What Prince Philip thought about being surpassed by his son is less certain: some thirty years previously he had played the minor role of Donalbain. On the few occasions when I saw the Duke I had the firm impression that he didn't like being outdone by anyone. This was one of those occasions; another, as we have seen, was at Cowes.

Eric Anderson has declared that Charles played the part better than any other amateur or professional actor he had ever seen. He had seen better productions but never a better Macbeth, he said. Well, now, maybe Eric Anderson was right, or equally improbably, he hadn't seen many Macbeths, but I couldn't help feeling that Charles's rank coloured critical appraisal of his acting by Anderson as it had with his trumpet-playing by Miss Kim Murray. In any case, it was hard for Charles to preserve a sense of proportion when attitudes towards him swung wildly from inverted snobbery and such petty nastiness as 'Charlie boy' to suggesting that he was a better Macbeth than Olivier and Gielgud. I like to think that my own low-key responses and rather less extravagant, but sincere praise earned me Charles's trust.

It might be thought that when Charles was a youth at Gordonstoun, miles away from the nearest town and hundreds of miles from Fleet Street, he would be fairly free from incidents. Far from it.

I recall a particular trip from Gordonstoun to Haddo House in Aberdeenshire where Charles and some other boys were going to give a recital. It was one of the last places to associate with any sort of dramatic incident. Haddo House is near the village of Fyvie and a couple of specks on the map called Crofts of Haddo, north-west of Aberdeen.

As usual we were travelling in the Land Rover. We slowed down after bowling along at 70mph where traffic conditions allowed on the main Elgin to Aberdeen road when one of the boys gave a yell. I pulled up.

Every single wheelnut on the rear nearside wheel was within an eighth of an inch from coming off. I broke out in a cold sweat when I thought what might have happened if the wheel had come off while we were travelling at speed. Eventually it was assumed that the trouble had been caused by faulty workmanship at a recent service. Nevertheless, I could not completely dismiss from my mind the thought that it might have been deliberate, if not done by somebone with malevolent intentions, at least by a boy with a poor sense of practical joking. Whatever the cause, the possible outcome stirred up my sense of vigilance. However, Charles and the other boys, with all the uncaring cheerfulness of youth, were quite unmoved by the incident. Charles certainly didn't lack guts.

There was another incident with the Land Rover which, although not physically dangerous to Charles, could have had serious consequences of a different kind for him. I was driving him from Gordonstoun to Balmoral at 4 a.m. – we always made a punishingly early start so Charles could get a full day there – when a roe deer, perhaps startled by the vehicle's headlights and engine noise, leapt over a fence directly in front of us. It was impossible to avoid it. The deer was thrown back over the top of the Land Rover and into the road behind us.

As soon as I had slowed the vehicle Charles jumped out and ran back to the deer, visibly concerned about the suffering animal. His Purdey shotguns were in the back of the Land Rover, bouncing about as usual. (His treatment of those superb weapons always made me cringe. He just heaved them in to take their chances with all sorts of odds and ends like wellington boots and tyre irons. It was much the same when we travelled by train: the Purdeys were heaved into the carriage as if they were lengths of old piping to be used for central heating. I felt it was like playing table-tennis with a Stradivarius for a bat.)

For a moment Charles considered shooting the deer to put it out of its agony. This wasn't quite as good an idea as it may seem. Although we were on a very remote road in northern Scotland, the sound of a gunshot at 4 a.m. would have produced people from nowhere, like Indians in a deserted-looking prairie in a Western. Gamekeepers, always on the look-out for poachers, would have homed in on the sound as if they were on radar. And Charles was often tracked by reporters at the most unlikely times and places.

Nevertheless, we decided we had to risk it and shoot the deer. Then we discovered that there were no cartridges anywhere in the vehicle.

Charles was very upset about the poor beast, for he realized that we were faced with the choice of two appalling choices: either leaving it to suffer, or despatching it as best and as quickly as we could. I picked up a large stone and went up to the deer.

This occurrence, too, brought me out in a cold sweat, and not just because of what we had to do. But if anyone had actually seen the heir to the throne's bodyguard clumsily putting to death a deer at four o'clock in the morning the headlines in some of the down-market papers would have been unimaginable. Nor does the effect on the large animal-loving section of the community bear thinking about. And on a purely personal level, I could have expected a stupendous rocket from Detective Chief Superintendent Perkins...before I was fired.

Charles's motives were irreproachable. Even so, I found

his concern difficult to understand, and perhaps typical of his sometimes paradoxical nature. He simply wanted to save the deer from unnecessary suffering, yet he frequently spent entire days doing his best to shoot them.

Another incident that could have had tragic consequences occurred one November evening when we were on our way back from Balmoral in the Land Rover. We had taken a rather roundabout route so Charles could do some of the driving, but when we got to the town of Keith I took over the wheel. Charles gave it up reluctantly: he enjoyed driving. The journey was uneventful until we got to the village of Duffus, where we had to turn right off a B road just past the picturesque church and onto the track leading to Gordonstoun. It was a point at which I always took extra care because normally there was little traffic and so children often played there. As I made the turn, from the corner of my eye I noticed a figure dart out from a car parked on the opposite side of the road, stand right in front of the Land Rover and point something directly at us.

There was a blinding flash, and infinitely quicker than it takes to tell, a dozen thoughts flashed through my mind before I realized that it was only a camera flashbulb.

What I did not realize was that the flashbulb had effectively blinded me for a second. Totally without warning I suddenly saw a child – a girl, I think it was – in our path. I swung the wheel round, and then straightened the Land Rover again. We missed her.

Charles turned to me sharply. I think he must have been looking away at the crucial moment and hadn't seen what had happened.

'What's the matter?' he asked me.

'Something in the road,' I replied, not trusting myself to say anything more.

Later I returned to the village and made enquiries, but no one seemed to know the man concerned. However, Bob Whitby was able to make a probable identification of him from my description. I wrote to Chief Superintendent Perkins at Buckingham Palace about the incident, minimizing it as much as possible, underlining nevertheless that photographers jumping out in front of our car and letting off flashbulbs in our faces like that could cause a nasty accident.

Whether the Palace subsequently had a quiet word with the newspaper concerned Perkins didn't tell me, but there were no recurrences.

For a long time afterwards, every time I thought of the incident I shuddered. Apart from the awful tragedy for the family concerned, if the less experienced Prince Charles had been driving and run down a child – no matter how blameless he was – an almost unimaginable furore would have erupted. Spiteful anti-Royals and sensationalists would have revelled in the situation.

Charles being who he is, 'popular' newspapers and their readers being what they are, he had only to be seen talking to a girl for a couple of moments for all sorts of overheated 'romance' stories to appear, with no shadow of a basis in fact. In my first years with him Charles was quite shy with girls outside his own family. In fact until he was quite a young man he could still manage to blush! But his lack of ease with girls was easy to understand. He had very little contact with them as a boy at Hill House and Cheam schools. When he was not spending time with his family, he was accompanied by a detective, which made it difficult for him to meet girls informally. (Later he had more opportunities.) So it was clear to me that he had no great desire to meet girls while at Gordonstoun. The fact that whenever the school maids passed him in the corridors or halls of the school they gave little giggles, snickers and simpers – no doubt out of embarrassment just as big as his – helped to suppress an inclination he might have had to get to know girls. Then, of course, there was the regime at Gordonstoun which, with its physical activity and copious cold showers, did *something* towards diminishing youthful sex urges.

As far as I could see, such interest in girls as Charles and his friends shared was almost exclusively theoretical and rather juvenile. Whenever we went to an outside function in the Land Rover – to recitals, concerts and school expeditions – we had the vehicle full of boys. Even on private family visits to Balmoral or Birkhall, for example, Charles might take one friend with him. There are a number of games very young people used to play to keep themselves amused on long car journeys: 'I spy', 'Beaver!' spotting car numbers and the rest. Charles and his friends hit on the idea of sizing up the girls we passed and giving them marks out of ten – long before the days of Dudley Moore's film 10. (Even after he had left Gordonstoun, Charles would occasionally make a mischievously joking remark about a girl's out-of-ten mark. In all the years I was with him, he gave a ten to only two girls – but more about that later.)

In any case, from an early age Charles was very conscious of his present and future responsibilities; he took them with an admirable seriousness. The furore over the cherry brandy incident brought home to him that he had to walk a very narrow line to avoid unwelcome publicity, although he was aware that he would never be free of it all his life.

Although it was against the school's rules, some of the boys at Gordonstoun used to slip away to a café in Elgin – Pete's Caff, I believe it was called – where they exchanged the usual badinage with the local girls. Of course, at this period it was all very harmless stuff; even so, Charles never joined in. Breaking the rules to meet the local lassies in public was simply not the sort of thing he would risk. Not because he lacked 'bottle': he was courageous enough, but for two reasons. As we have seen, he wasn't sufficiently interested in girls to be tempted to break the rules; second, he knew how the popular press would treat the story if he did decide to risk it and step just one inch over the line.

On one occasion girls from St Margaret's School, Aberdeen, were invited to Gordonstoun as partners for the school dance. I could imagine the frissons of excitement that must have gone through the girls at the thought of meeting and dancing with the Prince of Wales. (The song 'I danced with a man who danced with a girl who danced with the Prince of Wales' kept going through my mind at the time.) When the St Margaret's girls turned up they were rudely disappointed: Charles, accompanied by myself, had gone off to Birkhall for the weekend. Dancing was not high on his list of amusements.

There was another invitation to a girls' school, this time for a much longer event, and one that gave rise to strong rumours that the Prince had a secret girlfriend. When Gordonstoun decided to put on a performance of Gilbert and Sullivan's *The Pirates of Penzance* the school created a precedent by inviting girls from Elgin Academy to take part in the production. Until then Gordonstoun had followed the Shakespearean tradition of having boys playing female roles, but this was hardly practicable for an operetta. Charles, who had a pleasing light baritone, sang the part of the Pirate King.

During the period of rehearsals rumours began to surface that Charles had secret friendships with some of the local girls. According to these stories he used to sneak into an Elgin café to meet them. It was claimed that these stories were true because a number of people had actually seen him there with the girls. It baffled me how meeting girls in a café in full view of witnesses could be classified as secret.

Finally, one girl was actually named: Sandra Spence of Elgin, who played opposite him in *The Pirates*. It is true that they met offstage, but the circumstances could not have been more innocent and uninvolving. After the last performance of *The Pirates* Mr and Mrs Spence, Sandra's parents, threw a party for everyone involved in the production. It was hardly in the tradition of West End theatrical bashes: there were lots of tea and cakes, but positively no champagne or liquor. There were some thirty or more people at the party, including Sandra's parents and Bob Whitby (Charles's housemaster), so there were hardly any opportunities even for the boldest boys to get up to anything, let alone the careful, restrained Charles. But to cap it all, the girl he spoke most to at the party was someone else altogether: the daughter of a local farmer. No wonder Charles had a jaundiced view of the press quite early in life.

Nevertheless, the press – or some sections of it – persisted with the story that Charles had a steady girlfriend. Perhaps Sandra Spence found the stories flattering and provided cuttings for a scrapbook if she wanted to keep one. As for Charles, he said perceptively that denying newspaper stories would be pointless: people would believe what they wanted to believe, right or wrong. In fact he sometimes found the stories so totally inaccurate that we had to laugh about them. But that was then. I didn't want to spoil Charles's fun by warning him that he'd soon get fed up with fabricated stories to which he could never answer back. He found out soon enough.

Charles's career in the entertainment world was a very successful one at his level: the Duke of Exeter in *Henry V*,

Macbeth; then at Cambridge the parson in *Erpingham Camp* and his cabaret performances. As an organizer, however, he had one real stinker of a disaster, and 'stinker' is used advisedly. While still at Gordonstoun he was a leading member of the committee given the job of organizing a school dance to which young ladies of Aberdeen High School were invited.

Charles helped to organize efficiently the music, refreshments and other details. So far, so good. Then there was the matter of choosing a theme. At that time putting on a dance meant more than simply finding a suitable room with a floor that didn't trip up the dancers or stab their feet with splinters. The evening had to have a theme. In view of the local resources and the age of the dancers, clearly a theme such as the Rio de Janeiro carnival or a night in a Turkish harem was out of the question. Charles suggested 'fishing' as the theme, no doubt inspired by the local village of Hopeman where the seamanship classes he enjoyed were held, and by the practical consideration that he could borrow some gear from the fishermen there.

So, the main-dining room in Gordonstoun House was decorated with glass floats, creels and other gear and festooned with fishing nets. All very authentic. In fact, too authentic. As the evening got under way the temperature in the room rose as the young men and women danced with all the energy of the young determined to enjoy themselves. And the higher the temperature rose, the heavier became the the strong smell of fish. At first the dancers affected not to notice anything untoward, but eventually even the hardiest could take no more of it. Everyone escaped to the next room and danced round the buffet tables. The powerful pong in the main dining-room was a real wet blanket and passion-killer. It was like having a ball in a fried fish shop on a Friday night. But at least it was a memorable dance.

Charles's love of fishing nearly cost him very dear.

After he had taken GCE O-level examinations in July 1964 (he passed in five), when he was 15½ years old, he and a couple of his friends from school were given permission to go on an expedition of their own choosing until the end of term. If my memory serves me they were Charles Fforde and

James Smiley, and they – or at least Charles – decided on a fishing trip. On Monday 20 July I drove them all in the Land Rover to the Balmoral estate, where the boys camped in one of the bothies used by staff or guests on the estate, near the River Dee. A bothy is traditionally a hut or small cottage occupied by farmworkers in Scotland. The ones on the Balmoral estate were sturdy wooden structures which seemed to me to be rather Scandinavian in style. The one the young men occupied was well-kept and weatherproof, of course, but you would have to look hard to find any hint of luxury.

Later that same Monday we went on to Montrose to the Earl of Dalhousie's estate, where we were met by Mr Scott, the head keeper, and his assistant, Mr Gordon. Charles couldn't get into the River Esk quickly enough. He spent hour after hour waist-deep in the cold waters of the river. He went on fishing until 2 a.m., which was a tribute to Gordonstoun's physical toughening-up process and to his own stamina and determination. At least, that is what I thought then.

In the early hours of Tuesday morning we went back to Balmoral. The boys returned to their bothy, while I stayed at the home of the estate factor in the village, near the local shop. It was arranged that I would do a daily milk run from the shop to the young men at the bothy, which I did later that Tuesday. Charles and the others were already preparing to go off fishing again: keen fishermen don't believe in half-measures. They spent that day, too, fishing, supervised by the Balmoral head keeper Donald McHardy.

On Wednesday morning when I drove over with the milk, Fforde and Smiley were outside the bothy cooking a meal over a fire. I asked them where Prince Charles was. Still in bed, they told me: he wasn't feeling too well.

I found him sitting up in bed, looking flushed. Although he tried to play down his illness, he admitted that he hadn't slept very well and was feeling sick. In fact he looked quite ill, and when I touched his forehead it was burning. Clearly he was running a temperature. I wasted no time. I immediately telephoned Sir George Middleton, the Queen's physician. I told him who I was and reported that I thought Prince Charles was sick. This was at about 9.00 a.m.

Perhaps I didn't sound convincing or the doctor had no faith in a layman's diagnosis. Whatever the reason, although Sir George lived at Ballater, only some eight or nine miles from us, he still had not appeared after an hour...nor after two, and Charles seemed to be feeling rather worse.

Sir George's lack of urgency began to make me twitchy. He might have been fairly unruffled about the whole thing – after all, he'd had a great deal of experience in dealing with the sick, and keeping calm was a professional requirement – but as the time passed I became more and more agitated by what seemed to me to be an excess of calm and taking things steadily. So I tried to contact Chief Superintendent Perkins at Buckingham Palace, but with no success. I took a deep breath, and asked to speak to the Queen.

It's easily said, but for a young police constable, even the Prince of Wales's detective, it's quite daunting to say 'I should like to speak to Her Majesty.'

Suddenly I became really aware of what I had done : called out the royal family's doctor and then just rung up Buckingham Palace and said I wanted to speak to the Queen. For a horrible few moments I wondered if I hadn't over-reacted, and began to cringe at the thought of what my lack of judgement would bring down on my head. And then I remembered how seedy Charles had looked and had behaved. I knew he was always uncomplaining and determined not to show any weakness; he was the last person to stay in bed for nothing.

When the Queen came on the line I explained the situation and said that I thought it had warranted calling in Sir George.

Her Majesty agreed and said I had done the right thing. She instructed to me tell Sir George to keep her informed of the situation.

However, the doctor didn't arrive until about 11.30 a.m., 2½ hours after my anxious phone call. I was more than a little taken aback by the time it took him to get there; after all, I should have thought that the Prince of Wales was one of his more important patients, and when the heir to the throne is reported to need medical attention you might expect the doctor to get a move on.

Sir George examined Charles and decided that he needed a second opinion. This astonished me even more, but I had to assume that he had his reasons. Perhaps, when you're dealing with a Prince of the Blood you take no risks with any diagnosis more complicated than a cut finger, I told myself. But, in any case, I should have thought that the safest course to take was to transfer the obviously sick Charles to a hospital and get a second opinion there. Half a dozen of them, if they felt like it. Waiting for another doctor to journey over from Aberdeen meant a further delay.

Dr David Short, consultant physician of the Aberdeen Royal Infirmary, turned up at about 2.30 p.m., some five and a half hours after my initial telephone call. The two doctors consulted, and it was decided to have Charles admitted to the Watson-Frazer Nursing Home in Aberdeen, where he was diagnosed as having pneumonia.

While he was in the hospital, I quietly checked on visitors to make sure that the innocent-looking friends and relatives taking flowers to other patients were genuine and didn't have cameras concealed about them, and that they didn't lose their way and wander 'accidentally' into the wrong corridor. I also checked the presents and 'Get well' cards in case someone tried to slip something undesirable into his room.

There was one minor detail that had to be taken care of. Charles had been taken into the nursing home straight from the camp site at the bothy, and he had little more than what he was wearing when he was moved. So I bought a few things for him locally, and he was even measured for a suit while still a patient in case his own topclothes didn't turn up before he was discharged. In fact he didn't need it after all, for when his housemaster Bob Whitby and some of his school friends came to visit him they brought some of his own gear for him.

He was kept in for ten days before being allowed to return home to Windsor. We flew south in an aircraft of the Queen's Flight.

Later, while Charles was at Timbertop in Australia, I twice escorted the Queen on short trips. One was to Wimpole Street for a dentist's appointment, and another for a portrait sitting. During one of the car journeys the Queen asked me for my opinion as to what had brought on Charles's attack of pneumonia. She was polite and courteous, but it was a sort of arm's-length, strained conversation, and at first I couldn't understand why, although I supposed it was my fault.

Her Majesty, I eventually guessed, was not used to talking much to people at my level. When visiting a hospital or a factory, something of that nature, her questions to people in the workforce would necessarily be fairly stereotyped and not personal, and she could always move on if things became sticky. Now her questions were highly personal, concerning her own son. It seemed to me that she was treading a narrow line between wanting to know about him and not appearing to ask me to tell tales out of school, in more ways than one.

I told her I thought Charles had been working very hard studying for his exams and that he had been overenthusiastic in his fishing, spending so long standing in icy water.

The Queen seemed satisfied by my explanation, but although I was honoured to have the private conversation with her, it was not one of my most comfortable moments.

6 Timbertop and Afterwards

I suppose that Prince Charles's success – and it really was a success – in *Macbeth* meant that his year ended on a high note. Otherwise it had been a fairly uneventful year for him. He had become accustomed to Gordonstoun, had become integrated into the life of the school and was finally accepted by the other pupils as something more than a curiosity.

In fact the year was too uneventful, too ordinary. He had lived an active life from an early age: he'd had to, whether he liked it or not. Including Gordonstoun he had attended two boarding-schools; he had shuttled back and forth between a number of homes, which included a palace and a couple of castles; he had gone sailing and shooting on equal terms with adults. He told me that he wanted a break from Gordonstoun – a point he had made to his parents more than once, it appeared. University was still too far off to satisfy his need for the change.

In the autumn of 1965 I was with the Prince at Balmoral, where he was on holiday with his family. After my first visit there I could easily understand why it is the Queen's and Prince Charles's favourite residence. It is quiet and peaceful, and in the middle of some 50,000 acres of private grounds. Creature comforts are taken care of by a staff of about 120. The walls of the castle are thick enough to keep out cannon balls and inquisitive journalists. Once safely inside the castle the royal family can really relax. During their ten weeks' stay the major activity is hunting: fish, flesh and fowl. The dress is tweeds and kilts for those entitled (and brave enough) to wear them: but in the evenings dress is very formal: dinner jackets and long dresses and jewellery.

One of the staff there told me that when Charles was a child he enjoyed roaming the windy Scottish hills alone, playing pingpong with the servants in the Silver Pantry and 'helping' the chef, Ronald Aubrey. They are probably among his best memories of childhood.

I didn't know what to expect the first time I went there, and I was in for a surprise. The stone-flagged entrance hall has a statue of Queen Victoria in rather a grim mood, sternly offering a silent warning to the newcomer to be on his best behaviour while he is there. But also in the hall is an untidy muddle of waterproof clothing – it can rain in Scotland, even in summer – wellington boots that have been graced by too many blue-blooded feet to be called 'wellies' and a thicket of fishing rods. The other feature of the entrance hall are the dog bowls. The royal dogs are always fed in the hall.

On this first visit to Balmoral I was still a member of the uniform staff and I had my meals with the household staff in the servants' hall. It wasn't until later when I had become Charles's personal detective that I managed to get a good look at above-stairs. I found it to be a thoroughly medieval castle – a real Prisoner of Zenda château with a whole herd of stags' heads on the walls. I found their glassy stares quite unnerving at first.

The royal family had film shows in the ballroom, a vast space which seemed almost big enough for indoor football, to which the staff were admitted…as long as they got there before the family. Once they were seated no one was allowed, or dared, to sneak in. Our seats at the back of the hall were padded chairs but not the sort that were kind to the bottom after a couple of hours sitting down.

The Gillies' Ball, which the royal family gave for the staff, was also held in that ballroom.

Heavy with history as the castle was, it didn't touch me as closely as one night I spent in the Palace of Holyroodhouse, which was occupied by the Duke and Duchess of Hamilton at that time. When Charles took part in musical performances at St Giles's Cathedral in Edinburgh he stayed overnight at the palace while other boys from Gordonstoun stayed with friends or relatives.

In the morning I chatted with the Duke and Duchess at breakfast. The Duke talked a while about Rudolph Hess and his astonishing flight to Scotland during the war, when it was said he wanted to meet the Duke.

Then I was asked if I'd slept well.

Politely, I replied that I had, although in fact I had been rather restless and occasionally half-asleep, half-awake. Once or twice I'd thought someone was in the room with me.

'Nothing disturbed you, then?' I was pressed.

'No. Why did something happen last night?'

'Not particularly, not last night.....' The Duke went on to explain. The room in which I had been sleeping was the one where David Rizzio, secretary to Mary Queen of Scots, was brutally murdered by Scottish nobles who dragged him away from Mary's presence nearly 400 hundred years previously.

In fact the wall of the room in which I slept and the adjoining ones had been erected inside the room from the original wall some time later, to leave a sort of passage where the ghost of Mary, Queen of Scots could walk without hindrance and without disturbing the occupants of the room. That's a real sense of history, making alterations to a castle to make things easier for the resident ghost.

On the trips with Charles from Gordonstoun to Balmoral, when the Royal Family weren't in residence there, we almost always went to Birkhall, the home of the Queen Mother on the estate. Although very occasionally we stayed there overnight we were mostly day-trippers, starting out from Gordonstoun at the crack of dawn in the Land Rover and arriving at Birkhall for breakfast. It was a wonderful way to work up an enormous appetite. The return journey usually started before dinner, although now and then the Queen Mother would have dinner early so we could eat before we set off again. Naturally my meals were served in the servants' quarters, and they were invariably excellent. Gordonstoun's 8p-a-day meals couldn't compare.

The Queen Mother was absolutely charming, always. I met her for the first time at Royal Lodge at Windsor. She personally conducted me through to the servants' hall and introduced me to the staff. It was the sort of gesture that made me feel a foot taller, and entirely devoted to her.

But to return to that holiday at Balmoral in 1965. I had quite forgotten the conversation with Charles about his wanting to have a break from Gordonstoun. When Sir Robert Menzies, the former prime minister of Australia, arrived to spend a few days at the castle, it didn't occur to me that there was any purpose to his visit, and in fact I was hardly important enough to be told. However, after he had been there a couple of days, I was accompanying Prince Charles on one of his solitary walks around the estate when he said, 'I think they're going to send me to Australia.' Rather selfishly, I immediately wondered whether I should be sent with him, and if so, for how long.

'They want me to attend an Australian school for a while,' Charles went on. He seemed to regret having told me so much, and fell silent. I didn't bring up the subject again.

In November the official announcement was made that Prince Charles would spend a term at Geelong Church of England Grammar School in Melbourne, Australia's 'Eton'. It transpired that Sir Robert had recommended the school, in his own state of Victoria. It was arranged that a Geelong boy would spend the same period at Gordonstoun.

Although Charles was now seventeen, in some respects he was still inexperienced to the point of naïvety. The prospect of being shunted right round to the other side of the world for a few months was more than a little unnerving. He did not spell it out to me in so many words, but he made it clear that he feared he would have a rough time of it all over again, as in his first days at Gordonstoun. But this time it would be worse, much worse, for a number of reasons. The tough Aussie youngsters would be prejudiced against a Pom, and a royal Pom at that. Australians are no great respecters of rank for its own sake. When Charles, Prince of Wales, heir apparent to the throne, arrived their attitude would almost certainly be 'Who the hell does he think he is?' and 'We'll show the Pom what's what'. The inevitable electric storm of publicity and general curiosity that would accompany him would only intensify the antagonism and Australian natural xenophobia.

In fact it turned out that his fears were exaggerated, although a boy of his age could scarcely be blamed for having them. The general reaction in Australia to the news that Charles was going to school there was more amused than hostile. One Sydney newspaper – if it can be dignified with that title – wrote of Sir Robert Menzies' announcement to the Australian Parliament that Charles would be going to Timbertop:

Sir Robert's announcement raised a cheer from the House.

Shortly after the Prime Minister was carted away and committed, the Government Pineapple Whip (with crushed nuts) read the following announcement from Buckingham Palace:

'The decision was made shortly after the weekly cherry brandy binge in Gordonstoun dormitories.

'The Prince of Wales was delighted. He said it will give him a wonderful opportunity to meet up with some genuine Australians in their true environment.

'Also, it will mean a break from the family, who are giving him hell since he was caught smoking behind the Gordonstoun toilets.

'Prince Charles is studying Australian history and has already read "For the Term of his Natural Life" and the various sonnets on Ned Kelly.

'To imbue a sense of realism in the young Prince, he will travel out here in a mock-up of an old prison hulk...'

Irreverent, sarcastic and rather juvenile, but not hostile.

I had mixed feelings about going there with him, but in any event I needn't have bothered about trying to make up my mind whether or not I would enjoy the experience: I was told that I shouldn't be accompanying him. As soon as I heard that, Timbertop seemed suddenly attractive and I desperately wanted to go. And, not to put too fine a point on it, I knew I should miss Charles. I had seen more of him than anyone else, daily, for the past year or so; he was the person I spoke to and listened to most.

It was no wonder Charles was apprehensive about going. In addition to all this, it was his first trip abroad without his parents and all the psychological support their presence gave him. And he would be without my moral support, as I was not going with him. This may sound pretentiously immodest, but the simple fact is that, because of my job, I was the adult who was his major confidant and support. I suppose I was considered too junior an officer to take care of Charles in relatively hostile territory. He was accompanied by Detective Inspector Derek Sharp, and by Squadron Leader David Checketts, who had been equerry to Prince Philip and so was no stranger to Charles.

Geelong Church of England Grammar School itself is in Melbourne, but it was out of the question to send Prince Charles to a school in a town where he would have been the constant object of press and public curiosity. So, it was decided that he would go to the school's country annexe, Timbertop, some 200 miles north of Melbourne and 2,000 feet up Timbertop Mountain. When Charles was told that boys from Geelong were sent to Timbertop for a year's outdoor activities, he thought it was going to be just another Gordonstoun with an Australian accent. But, as he told me later, it was markedly different.

Life at Timbertop was much less structured and regimented than at Gordonstoun. Although there were a few masters there, the younger boys were taken care of mainly by senior boys, with masters being called in or referred to only in cases of emergency. The boys were given much more freedom to do as they liked. Some of their activities were hardly the sort of thing that went on at Gordonstoun: searching for precious and semi-precious stones, panning for gold and sheep-shearing. Charles was far from skilful at this last occupation. In his own words, when he tried his hand at shearing, he 'left a rather shredded sheep'. Someone has described the Timbertop regime as an exercise in getting to know people, which did Charles a great deal of good.

Despite the goodwill of the Geelong authorities, Charles was in a difficult position. He had been set work by Gordonstoun to do in Australia for his A-levels in history and French, but at the same time as a senior he had responsibilities towards the younger boys. In addition to accompanying them on the field trips into some pretty rugged country, he also taught the juniors English and constitutional history. The fact that he came straight into the school into a position of authority added to the inherent resentment of a royal Pom.

There was only one way for Charles to cope with the initial suspicion and antagonism: stand up for himself. By the time he left Timbertop he had completely won over his companions and made new friends. Nevertheless, when he talked to me about his early days at Timbertop, although he typically understated his difficulties and his determination to overcome them, it was obvious that he'd had a rough passage before he'd been accepted for himself.

In the end, Prince Charles had a marvellous time at Timbertop as his articles in the *Gordonstoun Record* of the time show: 'Almost everyone...enjoys themselves up here. One never seems to stop running here and there for one minute of the day, from 7.30 a.m. breakfast – no morning run, although there's worse to follow – until the lights go out at 9.15 p.m., having had tea at the unearthly time of 5.30 p.m. If you have done a cross-country at 4.45 p.m. and arrived back at 5.05 p.m., it's difficult to persuade your stomach to accept food.' The syntax may be uncertain, but the enthusiasm is unmistakable.

The camp was no place for faint bodies any more than for faint hearts. One seemingly never-ending chore was wood-chopping. This was essential '...as the boys' boilers have to be stoked with logs and the kitchen uses an enormous number. The first week I was here I was made to go out and chop up logs on a hillside in boiling hot weather. I could hardly see my hands for blisters....Each afternoon after classes, which end at three o'clock, there are jobs which involve chopping and splitting wood, feeding the pigs, clearing out fly-traps (which are revolting glass bowls seething with flies and very ancient meat), or picking up bits of paper round the school.'

As I said earlier, some of the expeditions were into some pretty rugged country: 'You can't see anything but gum-tree upon gum-tree, which tends to become rather monotonous. You virtually have to inspect every inch of the ground you hope to put your tent on in case there are any ants or any other ghastly creatures. There is one species of ant called Bull Ants which are three-quarters of an inch long and they bite like mad! ....At the camp site the cooking is done on an open fire in a trench. You have to be very careful in hot weather that you don't start a bush fire, and at the beginning of term there was a total ban in force, so that you ate all the tinned food cold.'

The final confirmation that Charles thoroughly enjoyed

his spell at Timbertop came when Queen Elizabeth The Queen Mother visited Australia during his first term. He was given special permission to go to see her in Canberra, and they subsequently spent a couple of days together in the Snowy Mountains. He asked his grandmother to speak to his parents about having another term at Timbertop. He had heard that there was going to be a school trip to Papua New Guinea during the school holidays, and he was keen to go on it, he told me much later. When the Queen Mother returned to Britain she was apparently a persuasive advocate, backing up her case with exhibits in the form of photographs; and the Queen was convinced that another term at Timbertop would be good for Charles. And so it was.

When I first saw Prince Charles on his return to Gordonstoun after those seven months in Australia I was totally taken aback. It was almost as if I had never noticed him before. From the moment I was appointed as his protection officer I saw him almost every day of his life, virtually from the moment he got up until he went to bed, so I really didn't appreciate the physical changes in him. Meeting him again suddenly recalled to me our first official meeting after my appointment as his detective. I had the clearest of memories of how the thirteen-year-old schoolboy looked, and the contrast with the eighteen-year-old young man was staggering. The boy was hesitant, shy, awkward and pudgy, with a childish round face that was unremarkable; the young man was neat in his movements, lean and fit. But the most striking change which had taken place over the years was in his face. I could see almost no relationship between that chubby-cheeked lad and this young adult.

In his first weeks back at Gordonstoun Charles was full of his time at Timbertop and his other travels. He showed me photographs of his trip to the other side of the world, like any returning holidaymaker with his seaside snaps. But these were rather special, because in addition to a fascinating trip to Papua New Guinea he'd travelled a great deal during the school holidays on the eastern seaboard of Australia, where he'd visited friends, gone fishing and played polo. Then the journey back to Britain at the end of his second term was by way of Tahiti, Mexico City and Jamaica, where he joined Prince Philip and Princess Anne at the Commonwealth

Games. Not your everyday school trip abroad.

Nor were some of the people he met the kind he'd normally expect to meet socially. Near Cairns in Australia he met a seventy-year-old aborigine who was the oldest living man to have been convicted of cannibalism some forty years previously. Charles said later that the man assured him that he'd lost his taste for humans, but he kept his hands behind his back.

He told me of two particular incidents during his travels which had obviously affected him deeply for their to have been outstanding in such a colourful ten months.

The yearly trips to New Guinea were to meet boys from the missionary schools on the island, which have certain ties with Geelong Church of England Grammar School. If he thought that some of the field trips at Timbertop were in pretty rugged country, it had nothing on Papua New Guinea. Apart from the unfriendly and difficult terrain, it wasn't all that far from the days when the inhabitants were headhunters who ate their victims. It was the first time Charles had come into contact with such a primitive society, and he found it totally absorbing, he said. It was on a visit to a village that he had what he described as a wonderful and moving experience.

The arrival of his party was heralded by native drumming, and as they got to the entrance to the village, the drumming stopped. The entire village was assembled, and Charles was greeted by shouts of welcome. Then the villagers began to sing 'God Save the Queen'. Charles felt quite choked. It was the most emotional experience he'd had, and he confessed to feeling tears in his eyes to see all these people, so far from Britain, singing the National Anthem. He'd never forget it, he declared.

The other important occasion was at the beginning of the journey to the island. Before the aircraft carrying the headmaster and some 30 boys took off for Port Moresby, flying over Prince of Wales Island – seeing an island which has your name must have some effect on a young man, even one as accustomed to honours and titles as Charles – it made a refuelling stop at Brisbane.

To Charles's considerable surprise a big crowd had gathered on the tarmac to see the young Prince. He was quite taken aback, for he'd never had a crowd come to see him on his own: his previous experiences of big crowds had always been with senior members of his family. His own inclination was to stay aboard the aircraft, but a member of the party – probably Squadron Leader Checketts, although Charles didn't say who it was – strongly suggested he get out and greet the crowd. 'I had to be virtually kicked out of the plane,' he said, with understandable exaggeration. (The mind boggles at the thought of the young heir to the throne sprawling onto the tarmac at the bottom of the aircraft steps after a boot up the backside from one of his staff.)

However, with the mental courage that he had shown so often before and has shown since, Charles walked towards the waiting crowd. Quite suddenly he was completely confident and since that moment he had never felt nervous in public. He said...

And yet...

At Gordonstoun, and later at Cambridge, I sometimes noticed that the too-ready frown was still there. Nervous he may not have been, then or later, but though there was a great deal more self-assurance in his manner, his basic shyness or diffidence was not far from the surface. In fact I think that shyness can sometimes be seen even today, despite the apparent easy confidence that his constant public appearances have given him.

There was one other part of his trip which Charles found impressive. In the back of beyond, at a place called Dogura, was an Anglican mission, and he was strongly affected by the work they were doing there. He wrote of his visit: 'I would like to mention how fresh and sincere I found the Church at Dogura. Everyone was so eager to take part in the services, and the singing was almost deafening. One felt that it might almost be the original Church. Where Christianity is new, it must be easier to enter into the whole spirit of it whole-heartedly.'

His admiration of the mission's work was only to be expected, for from the first days I knew him he was always a genuinely religious youth with a true faith.

Charles's return to Gordonstoun from Australia in September for the autumn term of 1966 was something of a minor triumph. We'd heard that he had distinguished himself at Timbertop and on his visit to Papua New Guinea, and while he was away Bob Whitby decided to appoint him as Helper of Windmill Lodge, which was Gordonstoun's quaint title for 'head of the house'. In this Charles – and Bob Whitby – was criticized for the same old thing that dogged the Prince all the time I was with him, and well beyond, from what I could gather. A lot of people put this appointment down to favouritism or sycophancy.

'I knew people would accuse me of favouritism,' Whitby said later, 'but I chose him because he was the outstanding candidate, although I don't think he ever believed that. He was one of the best heads of house I ever had.' This observation made me recall Eric Anderson's declaration that Charles's Macbeth was the best he had ever seen by any amateur or professional actor.

There followed an incident which highlighted two different facets of Charles's ambivalent character, a mixture of maturity of attitude and of unworldliness.

Two of the boys at Gordonstoun were caught in a rather serious crime. A great deal has been written and said about this particular incident, much of it quite inaccurate and some of it sensational.

One Monday night/Tuesday morning in November 1966 there was a break-in at a shop owned by Mrs Nora McKenzie in Forsyth Street, Hopeman, a village on the coast some three miles from Gordonstoun. Some reports said that the shop was part of the local garage, but this is not so: it was just a shop on its own. Cigarettes, lighters, chocolates and other property worth about £80 (at 1966 prices) were stolen.

It was hardly a crime that would have baffled Sherlock Holmes or Hercule Poirot. First, there were the solid material clues of a brace-and-bit and a screwdriver which were left at the scene of the robbery. Second, at about 5 a.m. on the Tuesday morning two separate witnesses saw two boys wearing anoraks and carrying rucksacks cycling fast through Duffus village, which is midway between Hopeman and Gordonstoun, going in the direction of the school.

(Incidentally, one writer has said that the two boys stole a set of school keys and got into the army cadet unit's armoury, where they took a rifle. They did not; nor did they take any hand-grenades or an armoured fighting vehicle. In any case, the idea of two schoolboys setting off on an armed raid on bicycles is rather mind-boggling.)

Inevitably the local police began their enquiries at Gordonstoun and quickly established a link between the robbery and the school. The brace-and-bit and the screwdriver were identified by Mr Napier, one of the masters, as having been stolen from the Radio Guild workshop. A pair of wirecutters, taken at the same time, turned up later in the locker of one of the boys whom I shall call Maguire. (That was not his real name.)

The Sunday following the robbery at the shop a Colour Bearer in Windmill House approached Prince Charles as House Helper. This boy, named Joekes, asked Charles for permission to look through the locker of a fellow-pupil, Denham. (Not his real name.) Joekes said he thought Denham had taken his school pullover. Charles hated the situation, as no doubt did Joekes himself, but Charles, for whom duty always took precedence over personal feelings, really had no alternative to giving his permission.

Joekes didn't find his pullover, but he and Charles found something much more interesting and damning. Among other items were two cigarette cases, four cigarette lighters, a brush-and-comb set and boxes of chocolates. All these were on the list of stolen property.

Charles was becoming more and more involved in something that he really wanted nothing to do with, but, as House Helper, he had a certain responsibility for what went on in Windmill Lodge. Backed up by Joekes, he was forced to question Denham. As the questioning proceeded, it became evident that Denham and Maguire were implicated in the Hopeman shop robbery. The crime was much too serious for Charles to be able to deal with it, and he reported it to the housemaster, Bob Whitby, who in turn went to the headmaster, Bob Chew. He handed the inquiry back to Bob Whitby.

The break-in was a curious mixture of total amateurishness and careful thought. At Gordonstoun all clothing and major movable property was labelled with the owner's name. To carry out their robbery Maguire and Denham 'borrowed' anoraks from two boys, haversacks from two others and bicycles from yet another two. None of the stuff they had with them had their own names on.

Quite soon Maguire must have realized that the jig was up. He confessed to Bob Whitby that he and Denham had broken into the shop, and told him where the rest of the loot was hidden. Sure enough, hidden in a hole among some small bushes in the grounds at the far end of the running-track, just where Maguire had told him, Bob Whitby found two rucksacks containing 2,500 cigarettes, boxes of chocolates, two alarm clocks, tubes of shaving cream, a tiepin and cufflink set and lighter refills.

Round about this time Detective Inspector Bews of the Elgin police contacted me. He informed me that, as a result of the information from Mr Napier about the tools, he was fairly sure that two boys from Gordonstoun had done the robbery and that one of them was Denham. I had no option now: I reported the situation to Bob Chew and Bob Whitby. I said that in my view there was only one course open to us: call in Inspector Bews. Before we did that, however, Bob Chew called the boys' parents and told them that he had no alternative to calling in the police. The parents agreed.

Bob Chew spoke to Maguire and Denham first, and then Inspector Bews interviewed them in the presence of Bob Whitby.

Charles spoke to the boys' parents and felt sorry for them. The boys paid back the value of the goods that the boys had stolen; nevertheless, not unreasonably, Bob Chew wanted to expel them. However, it was part of the Gordonstoun philosophy that senior boys enjoyed the right to express their views on what happened in the school, and their opinions were listened to. That doesn't mean that they were acted on, but at least the boys were given their say.

So, in his capacity as Helper, Charles went to Bob Chew and pleaded for the boys to be allowed to stay on at Gordonstoun. His argument was that it was far better for the school to keep them on, influence them by example and try to reform them rather than to discard them. It was, I thought, an adult and humanitarian attitude, but it failed to persuade the headmaster and the boys were sacked.

Of course, Charles hadn't appreciated the enormity of the boys' crime. In fact he found it difficult to take it in. Talking of the robbery, he told me afterwards, 'I didn't know people actually did that sort of thing. I thought it was only something you read about in books or saw in films.' He was eighteen years old at the time. As he was to say on a couple of rather more lighthearted occasions later, he did lead a sheltered life. I told him that life could be rougher and tougher than anything he might see on a screen.

There was a footnote to the incident. Once the story became public knowledge it was certain that some of the more sensational papers would want to work Prince Charles into it somehow. So Bob Chew had a word with someone at Buckingham Palace and a story was agreed upon by everyone concerned. According to the Authorized Version the matter was brought to the notice of Bob Whitby by direct enquiries by the Elgin police; Prince Charles and Joekes were not involved in any way.

Another story came out after the dust had settled. Apparently once the two boys, Denham and Maguire, were caught bang to rights they informed on all the boys at Gordonstoun who had been secretly smoking. Whereas the actual robbery raised no real ire among the other boys, the rumour that Denham and Maguire had grassed on them for smoking made their blood boil. There was a strong movement in favour of ducking the two boys in a pond but, as I recall, nothing came of it.

While Charles was at Gordonstoun he celebrated his eighteenth birthday, which, if had been a commoner, would have meant that he was at last entitled to vote. As far as he was concerned, however, this coming-of-age brought with it unique privileges and heavy duties. If anything happened to the Queen he would be able to reign as king in his own right without a regent. He became qualified to act as senior Counsellor of State in the Queen's place when she travelled abroad. He could conduct a meeting of the Privy Council and give the Royal Assent to Acts of Parliament. Finally, if necessary, he could declare war or make peace – although, of course, this would be with the advice of his ministers.

It was not until rather later that I truly realized the added responsibility that Charles's accession to great authority had placed on me as his personal protector. When he went up to Cambridge I was shown a memorandum from Philip Moore,

Assistant Private Secretary to the Queen, to David Checketts, Equerry to Charles. In it Moore said that he would be most grateful if the Prince of Wales could sign documents as Counsellor of State on a day when Princess Margaret would not be available. A box would be taken by car from the Royal Mews to Trinity College and, the memorandum continued, apart from the driver, of course, the box was not to be handled by anyone other than the Prince of Wales...and Mr Varney.

Before Charles's eighteenth birthday his parents tried to keep his royal duties to a minimum so as not to cause too great a disruption of his studies. However, he attended a few engagements, probably to ease him in gently into becoming accustomed to them. His first official public appearance was when he was sixteen–and–a–half, when he flew in from Gordonstoun to a garden party at the Palace of Holyroodhouse.

Some 600 young people, some Commonwealth students studying in Scotland, some Scots, were invited to the party given by the Queen and Prince Philip in the grounds of the palace. As Charles lined up with his parents to greet the guests, the Cameronians' band struck up 'Charlie is my darling', which he must have found excruciatingly embarrassing. I'm told that not all the guests were sure who the Prince of Wales was; they just shook hands and moved on with a vague smile. One girl didn't even do that and started to walk away.

'Hi, wait a minute!' Charles said. He stepped forward, his hand outstretched.

Not according to protocol, perhaps, but amusingly human.

There was one much more significant and solemn occasion which he attended soon after his sixteenth birthday: the state funeral of Sir Winston Churchill. The flight to London from RNAS Lossiemouth in a Heron of the Queen's Flight was unpleasantly uncomfortable because of appalling weather. In fact it was so bad that we had to return to Scotland by train. Charles was a little on edge – not because of the weather but because of the importance of the occasion. After all, he was barely sixteen.

'Still, I'm sure that everything'll be all right with Mummy and Daddy there,' he told me.

After the milestone of his eighteenth birthday he attended his first State Opening of Parliament; then he flew to Melbourne to represent the Queen at the funeral of the Australian

Prime Minister Harold Holt, and he was host with the Queen at his first Buckingham Palace garden party.

For more than 200 years the bells of the University Church of Great St Mary's had rung a special peal for the birthday of the heir to the throne. As Charles was at Cambridge for his nineteenth birthday he decided to climb the 123 stairs to the belfry to thank personally the dozen bellringers. It was a trip I could well do without, and when Dr Denis Marrian, Charles's tutor, began to follow him up the stairs I decided that I need not make the full ascent myself. I stayed part-way up the staircase, secure in the knowledge that there was no other way up or down. On Charles's return to ground-level there was a rather odd incident. One of the church workers stepped forward and handed him a rose that he had been given by Michael Coles of the BBC to present to the Prince. The point of the gesture still eludes me.

Charles was made Guardian (head boy) at Gordonstoun in his last term. Again there was generally no doubt that it was a deserved appointment. Charles was proud to have it and to maintain a family tradition: Prince Philip had been Guardian in 1938-9.

Becoming Guardian meant that Charles had graduated to having his own study, and he moved into a bed-sitting room in the small flat of Bob Waddell, the art master. It was crammed with books, odd objets d'art that he had collected, paintings and pottery. The place smelled – and looked – more like a studio than a flat with its persistent odours of clay, turpentine and paints. Charles enjoyed rummaging around there, enquiring about the various objects.

They had a another interest in common. Bob Waddell did most of the make-up for the school theatrical productions – reasonably enough, I suppose, for an art master.

Finally, Charles gained two A-levels: a Grade C in French and a B in history, with a distinction in the optional special paper. There would be some lively discussion about his qualifications and a spirited defence of his abilities.

The question now was where Charles would go next.

7 Trinity (1)

I heard from friends on the palace staff of how it was decided that Charles would go to Trinity College, Cambridge. It was one of the decisions that were made at a special dinner party a couple of days before the last Christmas before he went to Timbertop. It was a high-powered gathering, as befits a conference to settle the future of the heir to the throne.

In addition to Charles's parents those present were Earl Mountbatten, Sir Charles Wilson (chairman of the Committee of University Vice-Chancellors), the Archbishop of Canterbury (Michael Ramsey), the Dean of Windsor and Harold Wilson, the then Prime Minister. Sir Michael Adeane, the Queen's private secretary, was there but didn't join in the after-dinner discussion.

It is interesting to speculate what Prince Philip really thought of this intellectually high-powered gathering and the discussion. He once said he was 'one of those stupid bums who never went to university, and I don't think it has done me any harm'. Charles didn't forget this remark. Shortly before I was posted away from being his protection officer Charles said of himself that he was '...one of those stupid bums who went to university...and I think it has helped me'.

Charles, who was a month past his seventeenth birthday, was not invited to the dinner party and so had no opportunity to present his own views.

When invited to give his opinion Mountbatten had it all pat in his mind: Trinity College, like Charles's grandfather; Dartmouth like his grandfather and father and then to sea in the Royal Navy with a command of his own. This was a fairly safe and established career structure.

Charles, in many matters a traditionalist – he was by no means a reactionary, as some of his exploits at Cambridge later were to show! – wanted to go to Cambridge rather than a redbrick university, he told me. Apart from other considerations, there was the family connection with Cambridge, and it had the strong advantage of being reasonably near Sandringham, where a cottage on the estate had been converted for his use.

Once it was agreed that he would go to Cambridge the college had to be chosen. The Dean of Windsor was given the task of visiting some heads of colleges, and he produced a short-list of five colleges, finally coming down in favour of Trinity, his own college, where his elder son Robert was an undergraduate. Charles knew Robert, and Edward, the Dean's younger son, would be a freshman at Trinity at the same time as himself.

The Master of Trinity was Lord ('Rab') Butler, considered by many who should know to be 'the best Prime Minister we never had'. Very possibly he would have been a good premier, but on one occasion he displayed all the tact of an American football linebacker. Subsequently he gave a newspaper interview in which he said: 'Quite frankly, you know, the Queen and the Duke are not university people – they're horsey people, commonsense people. [Ouch!] The Queen is one of the most intelligent people in England and brilliant at summing up people, but I don't think she's awfully interested in books. You never see any lying about her room when you go there, just newspapers and things like that. Whereas Prince Charles has a tremendous affinity for books – they really mean something to him.'

Perhaps it's just as well that Lord Butler said that after it had been decided and was made generally known that Charles was going to Trinity! There would be one departure from tradition in Charles's time at the college. The two King Edwards and George VI had not stayed at university for the full three years. Charles was quietly very pleased with his examination successes at Gordonstoun – particularly in view of the interruptions to his studies – and I was fairly sure that when the time came he would eventually try for a degree.

However, when it came to deciding on what he would study at Trinity, it wasn't quite straightforward. A lot of people didn't want him to try for a degree; his father felt that Charles shouldn't be absolutely bound to take a degree, while one or two advisers said quite positively that he shouldn't be *allowed* to take any examinations.

But as I could have told them, when Charles made up his mind to do something, he'd made it up. He was determined and dogged as a youth and he was growing up into an equally resolute young man. He didn't want anyone to think he was dodging the sort of public judgment that all other students and undergraduates have to accept. He was ready to stand up and let himself be counted.

Charles decided to take the Part I Tripos archaeology and anthropology degree course for his first year of study, with the option of changing over to history for Part II.

There were two important departures from tradition to set a precedent. Because, as I have said, none of Charles's three student forebears had stayed at university for the full three years they had not taken a degree, so he was going to be the first heir to the throne to try for one. If he failed, he would be the butt of all sorts of sly remarks and cruel jokes. It was a bold step to set such a precedent, and typical of the man.

During the conversation Charles had with me about wanting to get away from Gordonstoun for a spell – this was just before it was decided he would go to Timbertop – he mentioned that when he went up to university he wanted to live in college. This was indeed flying in the face of the royal family's Cambridge tradition. His grandfather (George VI) and great-great-grandfather (Edward VII) had both been at Cambridge, but they lived in houses and their tutors came to them: the mountains came to Mahomet. Charles's great-uncle Edward VIII had lived in college at Oxford, but in view of his reputation there as a *bon viveur* it was unlikely that the royal family could think him a model to be copied. Not that Charles was likely to anyway. From odd remarks he made to me, it was pretty clear that he was looking forward to a last chance of some tranquillity with a minimum of royal duties to carry out. 'I'll never have the time to do the studies I want to once I've left university,' he said once.

My first reaction when I knew I was going to continue as

Prince Charles's detective at Cambridge was one of pleasure and satisfaction. While he was in Australia I filled in for other Royal Protection Group officers who were taking leave or absent sick: I performed fairly routine duties with different members of the royal family, much as I had done before I became the Prince's detective. I even had the honour of guarding the Queen on a couple of occasions. I was enormously proud to be given the duties, of course. Nevertheless, being assigned to different royals on an *ad hoc* basis lacked the personal element of my work in Charles's service.

It didn't occur to me then, but later I realized that the heir to the throne was the man I knew best and was closest to. For five years no one had been closer to me; my own circle of acquaintances had shrunk to virtually one person. If I'd had to do another job, it would have meant starting absolutely from scratch with a group of entire strangers. That was a problem that I should not have to face for a while; and to be honest, I didn't even think of it at the time. When I finally did, it was traumatic.

After enjoying the initial euphoria at the prospect of accompanying Charles to Cambridge, I began to be concerned. His security would be a problem.

The most worrying thing was the sheer geography of Cambridge itself. Gordonstoun was remote, and the surrounding area was thinly populated. The school and its grounds were fairly isolated: outsiders could not easily intrude into the private estate. When Charles went to Australia, he was deliberately sent to Timbertop to keep him away from the town, so that he wouldn't be subjected to the attention of people who would treat him as a sort of curiosity at best and a sideshow at worst. It also kept him away from the weirdos and nutters to be found in any society.

George VI, Charles's grandfather, wanted to live in college, but his father George V and his very regal mother Queen Mary would have none of it. George was installed in a rented house some distance from the college, which meant that he wasn't able to mix with his fellow undergraduates – and at that time he wasn't even heir to the throne. A similar situation with Charles would have made life much easier for me, but he was determined to mix with the other students as much as was possible and was wise.

Once it was decided that Charles was going to Trinity, in the June of that year I went to the college with Chief Superintendent Perkins to reconnoitre the territory, as it were, and see what my problems were going to be. Or in other words, I went to case the joint.

One of my major problems was that at Cambridge Charles would be living right in the middle of a town, mixing with people in the streets, in a college where almost anyone could walk in at any time during the day. He would be vulnerable to simple accidents, such as being knocked off his bike by a car.

And then there were women. At Gordonstoun there were no girls, twice daily cold showers and lots of exercise. (Nor did Timbertop offer any female temptations.) While he was at Gordonstoun Charles had the average sixteen- or eighteen-year-old boy's interest in girls – which wasn't much in those days.

Cambridge would be a very different matter. Charles would be the natural target for any number of young women; after all, apart from being Prince of Wales he was a very presentable young man. And he was growing up. True, he was still basically shy and inclined to to be introverted then, but that would only make him more attractive to many girls less shy and restrained than he was.

By the time we went to Cambridge, a subtle change had grown in the relationship between Prince Charles and myself. This was not simply the result of our spending so much time together, nor was it only because of his increasing formal education and knowledge of life. I was nine years older than Charles. When we were twenty-two years old and thirteen years old respectively those nine years were enormous to the youth. At 28 years and 19 years respectively we were much closer to being contemporaries: I no longer had the weight of years to give me authority. In our first years together Charles did what I asked of him simply because I was one of the older people who had to be obeyed; at the end of the Gordonstoun period, although he still followed my 'advice', it seemed to me that he did it out of a reasoned respect for my professionalism. So my influence remained, even though it was one of voluntary acceptance as far as the Prince was concerned.

But now we were venturing onto those most dangerous of seas that had wrecked countless well-founded friendships: relationships with the opposite sex. God knows that I wasn't the most experienced man of my age, although being a policeman can be a course in instant maturity. It was not my brief to keep him away from young women, and in any case I was privately all in favour of Charles's growing up like any other young man and enjoying himself, but I anxiously hoped that he could be diverted away from the wrong types...and that I could tell which ones they were...

I was concerned that he might accidentally get into awkward situations, like the celebrated 'cherry brandy' incident, or be drawn into ones that had been deliberately engineered. (I guessed correctly about that. He would be, all right!) Later I again became aware of the bond that had been formed between us. When I first went to Gordonstoun I was worried about another 'cherry brandy' incident because it would mean me losing my job. Now my concern was for Prince Charles, that he should not become involved in anything that reflected on him.

Finally, there was the problem – if I can call it that – of Charles himself. He was now nineteen years old and had always showed all the signs of complete normality. He was bound to be interested in women without any encouragement from them. Although he had come home from Timbertop very much more self-assured than when he left Gordonstoun, it was only an improvement on what he was before. Despite over-enthusiastic statements about his newfound confidence and lack of shyness, he was still shyer than most young men of his age; he was still relatively naïve in many respects. The undoubted physical maturity he had acquired in Australia and on his other extensive travels could be a handicap, for it made him appear more sophisticated that he really was. And he hadn't been mixing with girls in Australia, either. In Cambridge he would be much less closely supervised and watched over by teachers and equerries than previously. In these new surroundings, subject to pressures and influences of which he had little or no experience, he was going to be vulnerable.

Before Charles began his first term at Trinity he and his father had already inspected his room – or as it turned out, rooms: E6, on the first floor of one of the turrets which make New Court look a little like a medieval fort. The idea of putting him on the first floor was so that curious people wouldn't be able to peer through his window. My room was adjacent to the porter's lodge, which was on the same side of the court in the turret next to his. The room was about as large as a steerage cabin on a nineteenth century emigrants' ship and was a long, long way from the bathrooms. The only things in favour of it were history and tradition, but I would have cheerfully swapped them for comfort. Much more serious was that I could not see the entrance to Charles's staircase from my room. After I had been there for a short while I was thinking of getting myself moved to a room in the turret diagonally across the courtyard where I could keep a discreet eye on Charles's quarters. It was not to see if he Got Up to Anything, of course, but to make sure that he wasn't besieged by the curious or the awkward.

But then I had a visit from someone who gave me a tip-off concerning a possible real danger to Prince Charles. When I first heard it, my hair stood on end and I made immediate arrangements for the move. But more of that later.

The Queen made a private visit herself before Charles moved in, and interviewed at some length Mrs Florence Moore, who would be his daily cleaner, or 'bedder'. The college sick-bay and the nurse in charge, Sister Custerson, were also visited. I realized why the Queen was interested in the sick-quarters. From our brief conversation in the car as we drove to her portrait sitting when Charles was in Australia I knew that his bout of pneumonia had seriously alarmed her. Of course, at Trinity he would not be doing any field trips in the rough Scottish countryside and even rougher Scottish weather. And in any case, Cambridge was hardly in the wilds – geographically speaking, that is.

Soon after the Queen's visit a small army of workmen from Sandringham turned up with carpets, curtains and other home comforts. Charles also had a private telephone and a small kitchen where he could cook simple meals and make some decent coffee. The other students in college had to make do with a gas-ring.

Before I visited Trinity I learned that the freshmen shared communal baths and, I was told, in the mornings groups hurried across New Court with their towels and shaving-kit to take their turn at the washbasins. (I had to join the mass trek every morning myself – which was no fun in winter. At least I didn't have that to put up with at Gordonstoun.) It was obvious at once that the washing arrangements could present some very sticky problems. Again, it wasn't that I feared for an attack on Charles's life, but baths and washrooms are favourite arenas for youthful horseplay, and there would always be the possibility of some fathead provoking an embarrassing situation. I knew, too, that Charles would hate to have me hovering about in the bathrooms to protect him from his fellow-undergraduates. He would accept the situation from a sense of duty, but he'd hate it as something that would emphasize his difference from the others.

When it came to it, though, there was nothing to worry about on that score. The college installed a bathroom on his staircase, insisting loudly that one had been planned there for some time. Charles may have had to share it with one or two other students on his staircase, but it was a much more secure arrangement. A discussion about the installation of the bathroom and bathroom facilities in general provoked a comment from a don which I overheard: 'Why do they [the students] need bathrooms? They're only here for eight weeks at a time.' I took care not to get downwind of that particular don.

All in all, Charles's rooms were something like an ordinary middle-class living room, although the kitchen was more Earls-Court-bed-sitter. It had one unique privilege for a student living in college: the private telephone, but given Charles's position and responsibilities, it was hardly excessive. His accommodation was a long way from the luxury of Sandringham or his other address in London SW1, but at the same time it was infinitely more comfortable than Gordonstoun's spartan conditions. And my own oubliette.

I travelled up to Cambridge with Inspector Coleman and Charles's luggage to brief the local police before the Prince officially arrived at Trinity. I was already there when he eventually turned up a little late because his car had been delayed en route by heavy traffic. It was as public an affair as a well-publicized pop concert. He had been persuaded to arrive in a mini to emphasize that he was just another ordinary freshman, which he clearly wasn't. This was glaringly obvious from the fact that Lord Butler and Dr Marrian, Charles's tutor, were waiting at the college gate to greet him, facing a sizeable milling crowd of wellwishers and the curious; and his personal detective was waiting for him inside the college.

When the Prince's car pulled up near the gates all he could see, he said later, '...were serried ranks of variously trousered legs, from which I had to distinguish the Master and the Senior Tutor'. Tactfully he didn't mention the forest of female legs and thighs barely covered by mini-skirts. Charles unwound himself from inside the mini and was almost mobbed by the screeching gaggle of young women who chased after him as he walked toward the gates. He was rescued by '...several burly, bowler-hatted gentlemen dragging shut those magnificent wooden gates to prevent the crowd from following in. It was like a scene from the French Revolution.' Well, hardly. These natives were friendly.

Charles apologized to Lord Butler for being late, even though he hadn't driven the mini himself. This was an echo of his days at Gordonstoun. Bob Chew, the headmaster, never minded how the boys got to the school – on several occasions Charles was flown to RNAS Lossiemouth by Prince Philip – as long as they got there on time. Robin Woods, son of the Dean of Windsor, who was starting his third year at Trinity, had the task of showing Charles around the place.

So at last he was in. And now to work.

Prince Charles's arrival at Trinity was not received with loud and universal approval. Acclamation was intermingled with disapprobation: there were discordant jeers among the cheers. It was not that the critical students were particularly anti-Charles or anti-monarchy, except a few extremists. Paradoxically one of them became one of Charles's close acquaintances. Much of the noise was, I learned, a sort of involuntary reflex by some of the undergraduates. Students are traditionally anti-Establishment, anti-elitist and 'democratic', forgetting sometimes that they are elitist themselves in attending university. So, to demonstrate that in a fairminded, democratic way they were unimpressed by the arrival of the heir to the throne they criticized Charles or poked malicious fun at him.

Although Charles kept a public poker face despite some unpleasant taunts, I could see that he was hurt. The attacks which began while he was still at prep school had not thickened his skin and he felt the barbs. He was still suffering from the frustration of being unable to reply, and this was made all the worse because many of the criticisms were unjustified. The National Union of Students tabled a motion expressing 'concern for the hardship' Charles's parents might suffer if he didn't get a student grant. Even the National Union of Teachers edged in on the act with an adolescent jibe about the 'royal borderliner'. A group of sixth-formers at a Suffolk grammar school wrote to a newspaper accusing Charles of 'a blatant use of the royal prerogative' in getting into university; other students with the same, or better, qualifications could not get a university place, it was said.

Yet Charles was no dunce who was unworthy of being at university. I had seen how hard he had worked at Gordonstoun, and his critics seemed to have forgotten – conveniently – that his studies had been interrupted by the Timbertop trip. However, he was not without his champions.

R.M. Todd, Secretary of the Oxford and Cambridge Schools Examination Board, was reported in The Times as writing that: 'Prince Charles excelled in the optional history paper – 'the one that marks out the high flyer' as regards judgement, initiative and historical acumen. If a boy has done well in this paper – and the Prince got a distinction – it is a very good guide to university.' Six per cent of about 4,000 candidates had gained distinction in the special paper.

Todd went on: 'I consider that his performance was extraordinary, especially when you consider that he was digging about in Australia and that sort of thing. He has so many things to do that he must have worked like a demon.'

Which really should have been the end of that. But of course, it wasn't.

8 Trinity (2)

As early as his second week at Trinity Charles was invited to join the Cambridge Union – although I cannot recall that he actually ever did so – by the then Vice-President, Ian Martin. The invitation may not have been entirely unrelated to who the leading speakers were on that occasion. These young men were due to debate at the Hemel Hempstead Arts Festival, and they dropped the original motion 'This House Welcomes the Reign of King Charles III' in favour of 'Put Not Your Trust in Princes'. I suppose they thought it was amusing. I have often wondered how they would have reacted to a similar highly personal attack without being able to reply. It was a perfect example of people living in glasshouses throwing stones at a man with his hands tied behind his back.

At Cambridge Charles came much more into contact with the general public than he ever before. Gordonstoun was mainly a closed community. The majority of his excursions outside the school grounds were of one of two kinds. They were with a school party, properly supervised, or on his own to a private home, somewhere on the Balmoral estate or to friends of the royal family. Yet even on those private visits he had me sitting beside him, driving the Land Rover. And there weren't many people about in the Gordonstoun-Balmoral area outside the small town of Elgin. At Gordonstoun, too, he was a boy (in short trousers!) for most of his time there. At Cambridge he was a young man, somehow a more credible heir to the throne, a young man interesting and attractive to women; he was much more within reach of Fleet Street.

In Charles's first days at Cambridge I suppose I was a little concerned by the fact that he was going to be moving around the town in and out of crowds. Once more, the concern was less with his physical safety than with his reputation and dignity. However, Charles was usually very sensible and did without hesitation what I asked him to do for his own safety. We had established the ground rules of the protection officer/ Prince of Wales relationship at Gordonstoun and we kept to them thereafter.

The first public 'incident' occurred on a shopping trip soon after his arrival. He was accompanied by Prince Richard of Gloucester, who took Charles under his wing during his first days at Trinity and pointed out the locations of all the places in the town a freshman should know. The conducted tour was useful to me as well, of course, because I should be accompanying him on nearly all his journeys outside the college.

On this particular trip Charles went to a Cambridge store to buy himself an umbrella. Maybe he considered umbrellas lucky, as well as useful, after his experience with one at Timbertop. One night, after a stroll in the rain, he returned to the dormitory carrying that symbol of ultra-Britishness, an umbrella, which provoked shouts of 'Pommy bastard!' Charles was delighted, he told me when he returned to Gordonstoun: it meant that he had been accepted as one of the boys and not as a royal personage who had been foisted on them.

I don't think the sales assistant at the Cambridge store, Mrs Joyce Holmes, would have recognized Charles if the manager hadn't made an Olympic dash across to her and told her. He bought his umbrella, then spent a long few moments studying his change.

There are two kinds of people who rarely handle money. Charles was one of the fortunate group: he had money but didn't need to deal with it himself. Both at his prep school, Cheam, and at Gordonstoun he did very little shopping. Additionally, maths was his weakest subject. Nevertheless, he finally calculated that he had been short-changed and asked Mrs Holmes, 'Excuse me, but have you given me enough?'

Flustered, she checked and admitted that she hadn't. The change was £1 short.

This mistake was probably genuine, but my copper's professionally suspicious mind led me to believe that some subsequent 'incidents' were set up.

The next day, after the story of the purchase had been made public, the store sold out of all umbrellas, according to some reports.

Despite my misgivings, by and large all Charles's subsequent shopping in the street market went fairly uneventfully.

A couple of times a week he'd wander round, usually stopping at one particular fruit and vegetable stall where he could also get the brown eggs he preferred. I remember him there choosing with great care mushrooms to make soup for a meal when the Queen came to visit him in his rooms for lunch. Charles's favourite moments were always when he was alone, or with a minimum of companions, tramping the moors or fishing; just the same, he enjoyed his market days when he could chat informally with the traders. He felt that it brought him more into contact with everyday life.

Most of the time the Prince wore corduroy trousers and a sports jacket, which brought down criticism on his head from *The Tailor and Cutter* for '...following the cult of studied shabbiness'. But he was a university student, and he didn't want to stand out from his contemporaries. What was he supposed to wear for market shopping and going to lectures – morning coat and grey topper?

Accompanying Charles on shopping trips could present problems – for me, rather than him, because of his more-than-casual attitude towards money. There were no real difficulties while Charles was at Gordonstoun. I had a cash advance from the privy purse, and when we went on our rare shopping trips he did the selection and I did the paying, indenting later for the cash I had spent on his behalf.

London and Cambridge were a different matter, and Charles's attitude towards money was ambivalent. On the one hand he was careful enough about the £1 short-change; on the other there were times when I had the feeling that he saw me as an inexhaustible money-fountain.

One day I went to the palace to work with no idea of what the day's programme was to be. (This happens from time to time even in the best regulated of organizations.) As we got into the car Charles suddenly decided he wanted to go shopping for antiques in Kensington High Street. In one shop he selected a green onyx lion and asked the price. '£15,' the assistant told him.

'Mr Varney will pay,' Charles said offhandedly.

On the way to the palace I had called at the bank and had drawn out £10. In the sixties this was a not inconsiderable sum for a man with a police constable's salary. Well, I knew I had the £10, but as for the rest...I scraped together everything I had and handed over the £15.

I came out of the shop with 4½d, or 2p. Fortunately Charles decided against doing any more shopping that day.

There were times when Charles told me he didn't think it necessary for me to be in attendance. These included, for example, visits to his tutor, Dr Marrian, and to the Master's Lodge, private luncheon parties, lectures and meetings that were within the college grounds. There were also a few occasions with special circumstances outside the college precincts when he felt it was unnecessary for me to be with him.

During the day Charles usually cycled to lectures and tutorials outside the college precincts, and I followed in the Land Rover. It could be tricky, because there were times when he was in the middle of a swarm of cycling students. Trying to keep my eye on one particular student was like trying to watch one bird in a flock of starlings; driving through traffic at the same time didn't make it any easier. However, if we were separated for a moment at least I knew where Charles was heading, and I always managed to pick him up again quite quickly.

At the beginning I sat at the back of lecture halls, trying to look like part of the furnishings, but quite soon it became evident that not only did Charles not need me there – no crazed assassins were going to rush into the halls – but that my presence was a positive handicap to him. From the first day I became his protection officer I could see that both at Gordonstoun and at Cambridge Charles wanted to be just an ordinary student. Having his detective breathing down everyone's neck during the lectures only underlined that the one thing he wasn't was ordinary. So when he went to lecture halls or places such as the Wren Library and to his tutor's rooms I escorted him to the door and arranged what time to return and pick him up. These occasions were really the only moments during the day I could call my own.

Evenings were rather busier for me. Even when Charles stayed in his rooms in college I had to be within call in mine in case he suddenly decided to go out for some reason.

One of the places it was quite safe to leave him on his own once I had escorted him there was Prince Richard's house in Victoria Road, of course. As usual, before I left him anywhere, we always made arrangements for me to accompany him back to Trinity. No. 1 was an extremely unpretentious terraced house which Richard, Bernard Hunt, John Thomson and a couple of other architecture students had taken over when the house seemed to be held up by spit, string and hope. Externally unpretentious, that is. Prince Richard and his companions transformed the interior with a great deal of ingenuity and materials garnered from demolition sites and second-hand dealers. There were even some portraits of – I'm sure it must have been – Che Guevara. The few times I was inside the house I felt rather ancient and behind the times.

Inevitably Charles was bombarded with invitations to parties almost from the moment he arrived at Cambridge. These gave rise to some awkward problems. If he accepted all the invitations he would never had time to open a book. On the other hand, he didn't want to have the reputation for being stuffy, stuck-up or snobbish; and in any case neither did he want to be a hermit or anti-social. He wanted to play a part in Cambridge's social life.

Nevertheless, because of the demands on Charles's time, in addition to his studies and his activities with the Footlights Club, most of the invitations had to be refused.. Squadron Leader Checketts drafted two or three stock refusals which I typed out and sent off on Charles's behalf. One I recall was something like

> His Royal Highness the Prince of Wales thanks you for your kind invitation but regrets that he will be unable to attend.
> Yours, For and on behalf of
> HRH the Prince of Wales

One of the first of these refusals went to a Vivien Morgan and her flatmates Sue, Anne and Diana after Charles had been at Trinity for a week. Apparently the refusal was newsworthy, because the story appeared in a number of national papers, complete with pictures of the attractive twenty-one-year-old Vivien who was quoted as saying that she invited him because she thought he was goodlooking and that he might be lonely because he had been in Cambridge only a week. She added 'I hope it wasn't the bit about "with bottles please" that put him off.'

But that wasn't the bottom of the news barrel. That was scraped when the *Daily Mail* reproduced the note I had typed. I made a typographical error in copying out the draft: I typed 'invatation' instead of 'invitation' and the paper highlighted the error. Charles pulled my leg about it, but I couldn't help thinking that it didn't take a great deal to fascinate some people.

When it came to deciding which parties the Prince would go to, he usually accepted invitations from people he knew well personally and who were of much his own social standing, though not all. Some of the other parties would obviously be highly unsuitable for an HRH, even though most young men would have leapt at the undoubted opportunities that would be on offer.

One I recall in particular was a handwritten card which read:

Linda B...... Marylyn M.....[not Monroe!]
invite
HRH The Prince of Wales
to a
PYJAMA PARTY
on
21st October at .... from 8 p.m.
Please bring bottle and invitation.

'Pyjama Party' was written in emphatic red. I loved the last line. Clearly the girls hadn't been put off by Charles's refusal of an invitation which asked the guest to bring bottles, and while 'Bring a bottle' was understandable, the 'and invitation' was priceless. Did they think that Charles would have been turned away at the door if he didn't have his invitation, or that he wouldn't be recognized?

Perhaps Charles would have accepted *some* of these invitations if he had been plain Mister, but he was always conscious of the duties of his position and took great care to keep away from potentially embarrassing situations. (Or, more accurately, he *tried* to. Once or twice my blood ran cold at the thought of the possible publicity if he'd been caught out in a particular situation if I hadn't managed to extricate him just in time.)

As far as some of the other invitations were concerned, sometimes I'd make a discreet visit to the address and case the joint. It didn't take long to spot the places – and people – where Charles should most definitely not go, even though he might have had a right rip-roaring old time, and enjoyed it. From what I knew of him by then, I'm sure he would have.

There were a few invitations which appeared innocuous on the surface, but I got a whisper that tender traps were being laid for Charles. All good policemen have informers, even Royal Protection Group officers. One of mine warned me that the general plan at one party was to get him involved him in a game – fixed, of course – that would have left him with his socks and little else. They were seriously under-estimating his intelligence and determination – not to mention my own incompetence – if they thought they'd catch him like that, but the mere attempt could have been embarrassing.

Whatever the informants' motives for the tip-offs were, I was grateful for them. I like to think that it was because my informant had a sense of fair play and a genuine respect for Charles. After all, if a misspelt word by a junior member of his entourage could arouse so much newspaper attention, I don't dare to think what lively parties with Page 3-type girls who were not too fussy about their dress and who would try to encourage Charles to be the same would have done. He would only have had to put a foot inside the door for a couple of minutes for the story to push the outbreak of World War III onto an inside page.

Charles seemed to get little pleasure from most of the few parties he attended. The sort of party that he really had to force himself to attend was the cheese-and-wine, stand-about-and-chat and desultory-dancing party. He went to a number of them, again largely from a sense of social duty. However, hardly any of the parties he went to were successful as far as he was concerned. With the best will in the world, his presence did seem to be a powerful inhibitor on most of the guests.

Usually he would stand to one side of the room, a drink in his hand, although what was in his glass was anyone's guess – and in any case, he never seemed actually to drink any of it, and he never seemed to have a refill. I'm not suggesting that Charles was teetotal, but he restricted his drinking to a very modest intake of wine with a meal.

Although the Prince had this sobering effect on the evening, he was highly sought-after as a party guest simply because of who he was, and not for his potential contribution to the general jollification…and he was aware of it. It didn't help him relax. More than once he said to me, 'I think we'd better go. I seem to be putting a bit of a damper on things', or something like this. This was probably true enough. Nevertheless, I'm quite sure he was making a virtue of necessity: he was bored stiff with the party and was seeking an excuse to get away. He was much happier on his own, or with one or perhaps two companions tramping about in open country.

Charles was not a permanent wet blanket who didn't know how to have a good time, though. He enjoyed parties away from Cambridge: at Wood Farm or on the Balmoral estate, for example; and he had good times with friends near his own social level and background in Cambridge. However, he would always be very restrained when in public – unlike Princess Anne, who occasionally was quite extrovert.

I recall one particular evening when Charles and Anne went to see *The Four Musketeers* with Lady Susan Hussey and Nicholas Soames, who later became equerry to Charles. His sister Emma, if my memory serves me, was also in the party. Lady Susan, who became lady-in-waiting to Princess Anne, is the wife of 'Duke' Hussey, then of the *Sunday Times* and now Chairman of the BBC. Nicholas and Emma Soames are grandchildren of Sir Winston Churchill.

After the show the party went backstage to see Harry Secombe, who as a founding member of The Goons was always one of Charles's favourites. Already in a cheerful mood, we went on to L'Apéritif in Jermyn Street. There, under the influence of good food and wine, it became an even happier evening, to the point of becoming lively.

By the time Charles, Anne and the others were ready to leave, the press had gathered in force outside the restaurant. There was no sixth sense involved in their finding out that the Prince and Princess were having a supper party in a restaurant. Undoubtedly one – or several – of the L'Apéritif staff had made a discreet phone call to newspaper contacts to earn a few extra pounds. After all, the money would help compensate for their having to stay late to serve the royal party. When Prince Charles, Princess Anne and their friends go to a restaurant they're not going to be shooed out with 'We're closing now'; if they order something they're not going to be given a terse 'Chef's gone home.' Nor, for that matter, will the head waiter come to the table and say, 'Would you like the bill now? The staff are waiting to go home.' You don't start whipping off tablecloths and putting chairs on the tables round a prince of the blood royal.

When at last the party left the restaurant they were all in a state bordering on hilarious. Charles, as always, was the most restrained and self-controlled member of the group.

Then the transport arrived. The vehicle was nicknamed 'The Mighty One' because its registration number was MYT 1. Despite its impressive name and number, it was not one of the stately royal Daimlers, but a Vauxhall Cresta Estate. There were six of us altogether without counting the chauffeur.

When Anne saw the modest vehicle arrive she threw up her arms in mock horror and staggered back. I was standing behind her and she actually allowed herself to fall back as if she were drunk and incapable – which I knew she wasn't – and would have gone flat on the pavement if I hadn't caught her and heaved her upright again. I suppose her gesture was a mixture of practical joking and bravado, with perhaps an element of wanting to take centre-stage. In retrospect, I suppose it was flattering that she had that much confidence in me to know that I should catch her, but at the time I wasn't too sure of anything, and momentarily I had a bad case of wind-up.

Somehow we all squeezed into the car for the drive back to the palace. Once it was under way Princess Anne took a deep breath and said, 'Well, we made it.' Which could have meant that we'd all managed to get into the car or that the small Cresta brake had managed to get moving with such a heavy load.... Or that the stagger and mock fall display had gone off without disaster. Many a time after that I came out in a cold sweat thinking of the sensation it would have caused if I hadn't managed to catch Anne and she'd ended up on the pavement with all the photographers and journalists about. And as far as I was concerned I should have been fired from the Royal Protection Group quicker than a human cannonball.

It was a long evening. Our final call was to Lady Susan Hussey's home before arriving at Windsor Castle at 2.35 a.m.

Two of Charles's favourite social groups at Cambridge were the Wapiti Club and the Pitt Club. The first was a private dining club formed by Charles and some of his aristocratic friends. A wapiti is a stag, so the title was appropriate for an all-male club. Invitations that were sent out were formal, as was dress.

The club appears to have been fairly elitist. Charles's friends in it were Wykhamists and Old Etonians. They were wealthy and from old families. One of their outings, though, was definitely proletarian. They went to a working men's club to see *A Night at the Opera* – the Marx Brothers were Charles's sort of comics. As the film was at a private club, he had to be signed in, and to preserve his anonymity he gave the name Charlie Chester. He later explained to some of us that one of his titles was Earl of Chester, so he was perfectly entitled to call himself Charlie Chester. He also enjoyed giving himself almost Goonish names. When booking sleepers on night trains from Aberdeen or Inverness he sometimes used the name Postle.

The Pitt's membership was similar to that of the Wapiti, and it was a favourite haunt of some of the wealthier members of the university. Its membership was select and fairly intellectual, which isn't to say that it was like the Athenaeum. Many members were in a noisily cheerful frame of mind by the end of the evening, and there was a cabaret to help liven them up.

Charles, however, never forgot his position and drank very sparingly as usual. Although many of his friends might stagger a little, speak loudly, or be 'tired and emotional', he was always in total control of himself. This was not from any sense of priggishness or piousness: it was simply that he never, ever, forgot that he was heir to the throne and the importance of maintaining the dignity of the rank.

So Charles wasn't an enthusiastic partygoer – at least, not with strangers. He still had not overcome his basic shyness even though he managed to conceal it by a determined effort of will; his strong sense of duty and awareness of the demands of his position also forced him to overcome it. Nevertheless, in his early days at Cambridge at least there was still a marked diffidence about him, and for my part I tried to encourage him to be a little more self-assertive.

There was an occasion when we were invited to a cocktail party at Peterhouse by Jean Reddy, who ran the Haddon Library, where Charles did a great deal of his studying. The library was named after Alfred Cort Haddon, one of the founders of modern British anthropology. For some thirty years he was almost the sole exponent of anthropology at Cambridge, and it was due largely to his work and teaching that the subject gained its place as an observational science. Haddon wrote more than 600 publications.

Charles, genuinely regretful, told Jean, 'I'm afraid we'll have to miss it, because I won't have time to change. I'll be coming straight out of lectures.'

'Oh, that's fine,' she told him. 'It's quite informal. Wear what you like.'

Jean Reddy was formerly a nun, and an ex-nun librarian

might sound like a rather serious young lady. In fact she had a tremendous sense of humour, and maybe we should have been a little wary of her. When we turned up wearing sports jackets and flannels we found that everyone else was wearing evening dress, ready to go on to some other function after the party.

Charles took one look and turned tail. 'Oh, God,' he said. 'We can't go in there.'

I made the most of the situation.

'Look,' I said. 'You're the Prince of Wales. You're right, and everyone else is wrong. Just walk in and prove it.'

He hesitated, and I could read his thoughts quite clearly: '*I'll feel so awkward.*'

'Make them feel overdressed and awkward, because *you're* in the right.'

Charles shrugged and seemed ready to turn away. He checked, smiled, and then laughed. 'Come on, Varney,' he said, and walked in with seemingly total assurance. I could have cheered him.

There was another proof of Charles's increasing self-assurance – even though it wasn't total yet – and his waning shyness when he attended the Royal Film Performance of *Romeo and Juliet* while he was at Cambridge. As is usual, a number of artistes, directors, producers and other film people were presented to the royal family after the screening. The Queen, Prince Philip and Charles moved along the line exchanging a few words with the showbiz personalities, then the Queen and Philip stopped when they realized that Charles was no longer with them. He was some way behind them, animatedly chatting to one of the actresses: Joan Collins – who, needless to say, had not played Juliet. Charles's parents signalled to him to hurry up, but he stood his ground for a few moments, still talking to Joan, before joining them. I had the impression that the Queen was rather miffed.

Years after the sports-jacket incident I saw a photograph of the Prince arriving at the Cumberland Hotel for the annual dinner of the Master Tailors' Benevolent Association. *The Tailor and Cutter*, frequently quoted by the national press, had criticized him for 'following the cult of studied shabbiness' and for his fondness for sports jackets. Charles turned up for the dinner wearing an immaculate full-dress shirt with an order across it, waistcoat and trousers...and a sports jacket. He learned more than anthropology and archaeology at Cambridge.

9   *Bombs and Other Alarums*

At Trinity Charles continued the uphill struggle which began at Gordonstoun to be just another student. He dined in hall with other undergraduates, yet he found it something of a strain.

It was almost certainly because of this that the majority of his friends at Cambridge were close to his own social level and background: what Lord Butler is reported to have described as 'conventional hunting and shooting types'. Well, in many respects, that is just what Charles was, and so he felt easiest with birds of his own feather.

There was one exception, though. Charles's E Staircase was known by Trinity men as 'the Welsh Staircase'. Apart from Charles, Prince of Wales, here were three other occupants with Welsh names in rooms there. One of them was the long-haired, brilliant president of the Trinity Student Union, Hywel Jones, the son of a Welsh Nonconformist minister in a mining community. On the face of it, Charles and Jones were an ill-assorted couple, yet they got on extremely well together. Charles always had a very enquiring mind, and Jones must have been able to open doors onto ideas and social conditions from which the Prince had been shut off all his young life. From what he said before going up to Cambridge it was obvious Charles realized that this would be his last chance to be his own man – or at least, as far as that was possible for the heir to the throne. Once he left Cambridge he would never again be able to mix freely with people outside his own small upper-class circle. So, during this short period of relative freedom he inevitably was interested in the passionately held views of an intelligent young man whose background was diametrically opposite to his own. And as we have seen in more recent years, his concern for the underprivileged is genuine.

My responsibility was, as always, of course, for Charles's safety and dignity. As long as Jones didn't lead him into any public mischief or demonstrations that would would attract media attention, there was no reason for me to be concerned about the relationship.

However different their politics were, Hywel Jones's friendship with Prince Charles was totally genuine, his sense of right and wrong impeccable. I learned that a newspaper offered Hywel a handsome fee for a series of articles 'My Friend Prince Charles'. He sent the newspaper's representative packing.

Then one day a girl came up to me and asked to speak to me privately. I shall call her Mary, although that was not her real name. She was nineteen years old, and although she dressed like a refugee and wore no make-up I found her most attractive. Not to put too fine a point on it, I fancied her. Nevertheless, I was wary of her, for a number of reasons. Already I'd had young and not-so-young women apparently interested in me personally, and there would be a lot more approaches in the future. I was well aware that it wasn't my own charm they found so irresistible: they just wanted to get close to Charles through me. Then there was the disadvantage that she was on my own doorstep, which was no place to have an affaire – particularly as I was so close to Prince Charles. If any mud happened to fly in my direction some would inevitably hit him. As a matter of fact, my own conduct had to be as circumspect as his own, which was very irksome and made me appreciate his problems – although he had solutions that I didn't have.

So when this latest charmer sidled up and said she wanted a confidential word with me I said I was pretty busy.

'I'm a friend of Hywel Jones,' Mary said. That seized my attention. I led her into a quiet corner.

'Hywel is going to make a gesture,' she said vaguely. I felt like making one myself. 'A sort of public statement,' she went on.

'To the press?' I asked. 'What's he going to say?'

'No, nothing like that,' she said, looking at me as if I were rather thick. 'A *gesture*. He's going to put a bomb on Charles's staircase. It's as a protest against privilege.' The logic of this escaped me but I didn't pursue the matter. I was much more concerned with the immediate problem of preventing Prince Charles being blown up. I took the warning very seriously, for in the past Welsh Nationalists had bombed or set fire to government installations – and later they attacked holiday homes in Wales belonging to absentee Yuppies. To be truthful, I didn't believe that Jones would want actually to *kill* Charles, but I didn't know how much expertise he had with bombs. He might well do much more damage than he meant to.

I began to question the girl closely. She couldn't give me any precise details but insisted that Jones had told her a number of times that he was going to blow up E Staircase. But when, how and with what she had no idea.

I could see three possible explanations for her coming to me. First, that there actually was a bomb plot, that she'd had a row with Hywel Jones and that now, like countless women before her, she was getting her revenge on him by informing. Second, exactly the same revenge situation but there was no bomb; she merely wanted to make things as uncomfortable for him as possible. Third...well, that explanation came to me later.

I worked the conversation round to Jones, but as far as I could make out, she hadn't broken up with him: there were no signs of any animosity towards him. When I started criticizing him she actually defended him to me. Was it possible that she had a conscience, or could it be that she wanted Jones stopped before he got into real trouble? As the conversation developed, it slowly dawned on me that she wasn't really all that close to him after all. It was all rather Alice in Wonderland, but she kept coming back to the same story: Hywel Jones was going to put a bomb on E Staircase. Then at last she said something that put the whole thing into perspective. She said she could keep in touch with me and be a good source of information.

At last her true possible motives started to become clear to me: there could be several. She might have wanted to become briefly famous by having her name in the papers in a sensational bomb story: something like 'Girl Student Reveals Charles Bomb Plot! Mary X's own story...'. Or she could be one of those people who want to inform to the police simply for the thrill of being 'on the inside'. Someone once said that every man dreams of being a spy. So do some women, I suppose; and being a secret informer is about as close as they can ever get to it.

There was always the possibility that she was a sort of Royal 'groupie' and that Prince Charles's detective was a legitimate substitute, but for the reasons I have just mentioned that sort of relationship simply wasn't on. Unfortunately.

So, on the surface of it, the whole story was a false alarm. However...

Then she said something that jolted me: 'If you don't go to the local police and tell them, I shall.' Involving the local police and questioning Hywel Jones could have started all sorts of stories and wild rumours, exactly the sort of thing we were all trying to avoid.

'Fair enough. You do that.' I said. 'As long as you're aware of Section Five of the Criminal Law Act, 1967.' As it happened, that Act had been passed fairly recently, and I'd read it. 'Wasting police time can get you eighteen months, a fine of £500 or both.' In fact I was wrong on both points then. When I checked later I found that the maximum penalties were six months and £200; but I didn't think Mary was going to argue the point.

So that was that. Nevertheless, it wasn't the sort of thing I could ignore entirely and for a long time afterwards I was on tenterhooks, keeping an eye on Jones and nipping up and down E staircase much more than was necessary.

The bomb was entirely the product of Mary's imagination, of course. Yet there was nearly a development that would have been rather more explosive than a bomb. Charles became so interested in Jones's arguments that he contemplated joining the University Labour Club. Fortunately he asked the High Tory Lord Butler's opinion of the move. It must have been a fascinating discussion. Needless to say, the Master put the stopper on that idea.

I had more or less forgotten about Mary's bogus warning

of Hywel Jones's alleged plot to blow up E Staircase when there was an official announcement about Charles just before his nineteenth birthday. He would attend the University College of Wales at Aberystwyth to study Welsh, preparatory to his investiture as Prince of Wales. This news was received badly in Welsh extremist circles, which alerted me to the possibility of some Welsh hotheads making an ultra-nationalistic gesture. One evening I was looking out of my window across New Court towards Charles's rooms when I noticed two rather scruffy young men going towards his staircase. Obviously I could not know all the 6,000-odd students in residence at the university, but these two slightly furtive young men somehow seemed not to belong.

As I hurried across the fifty yards to Charles's corner of the court they appeared to be more sinister with every step. I met them on the stairs on their way out again. Close up, they seemed rather less threatening, but their accents immediately betrayed that they were Welsh. Still, they didn't look particularly guilty of having done anything. I discovered from Charles a few moments later that they were students from Aberystwyth who had come to Cambridge to collect money for their Rag Week.

'We were in Cambridge and we thought we'd come and see what you were like,' one of them had said unblushingly. Charles told me he gave them a contribution and they left, their curiosity satisfied.

Some time later, in December 1968, there was a second bomb scare. This was a real one, and the implications were serious. It occurred just before Charles was due to go to Cardiff to chair the Steering Committee for Wales Conference on 'The Countryside in 1970', followed by his attendance at Aberystwyth and then his investiture. The alarm was raised when bombs wrecked two giant water mains at Hagley in Worcester which supply Birmingham with water. Welsh extremists were strongly suspected of being the perpetrators.

Then a cryptic message was received at a Welsh police station.

It made no direct threat against Charles, but there were three worrying elements in the brief message: he was mentioned by name, Trinity College was referred to, and a time was given, the early morning. The Welsh police immediately contacted Scotland Yard, who called me as the man on the spot and the Cambridgeshire police.

Police cars and a heavy contingent of uniformed officers arrived to search the buildings and grounds. I couldn't help speculating whether Mary – Hywel Jones's self-styled girlfriend – thought it had anything to do with her 'warning' to me. Anyway, we found nothing, and the few extra plain-clothes detectives who remained temporarily were not there for long, because Charles left within a couple of days for the Christmas vacation.

Even though it was a false alarm, it strongly reinforced the doubts of a number of people about the wisdom of sending Charles to Aberystwyth, particularly as the Welsh Language Society, which had staged sit-ins at BBC studios in Wales, said they were planning a big protest against the investiture with a rally in Caernarfon on St David's Day.

It was clear that the Aberystwyth venture and the subsequent investiture could turn out to be unpleasant experiences, if not worse, for Charles. A number of important people tried to dissuade the Palace from sending Charles to the University College of Wales. He himself was aware of the possible perils and wasn't looking forward to going. Nevertheless, once again he dug in his heels and courageously prepared to face the situation without flinching. You had to admire him.

In the introduction to this book I mentioned that Prince Charles had a talent for getting himself into situations that were potentially highly embarrassing or even physically dangerous. He managed to get himself into hot water or to become the centre of unwanted attention in three different ways. First, by being dragged in by his companions, albeit with the best of intentions. Second, when he was the victim of other people's machinations. Third, by walking into situations of his own accord without realizing the possible repercussions, as in the cherry brandy incident.

In the first category of incidents, possibly the closest call, which was dangerous on both counts of embarrassment and physical violence, occurred one night in Cambridge when we were leaving the Pitt Club with a group of Charles's friends.

A word about Pitt Club. I had close contact with the cabaret artistes on the occasions I accompanied Charles to the club. This was because I spent most of my time in the club kitchen, which also served as a dressing-room for the cabaret artistes. One I recall in particular: a well-built belly-dancer. (I did say the Pitt Club wasn't like the Athenaeum.) Now, a belly-dancer might well be stimulating when she performs, out of reach, accompanied by exotic music on a stage with subdued pink lighting; close up in a kitchen, surrounded by cooks heaving pots and pans about and waiters screaming for their orders and not giving her a second glance, 'Fatima' can abruptly become Mabel Earnshaw from Otterly wearing funny clothes. Nevertheless the belly dancer at the Pitt Club still looked good even under adverse circumstances. I was sorry I didn't have a chance to get to know her better – that was the story of my life with women at that time – but with all the noisy activity going on around us, 'chatting her up' would have meant shouting loudly at her across the kitchen.

I was told that there were occasionally strippers at the club, but in those days they were rather more decorous than today's private club performers, and I don't suppose that the sight of a nearly-nude young woman would cause the heir to the throne any deep-seated psychological traumas anyway.

One of Charles's friends was the then Viscount Ipswich: James Oliver Charles FitzRoy, later Earl of Euston and heir to the Duke of Grafton, and a member of an ancient aristocratic family. He had been a Page of Honour to the Queen a couple of years previously, which was how he and Charles met, I suppose. He was a year older than the Prince, and was educated at Eton and Magdelene College, Cambridge like his father. He was tall, fairheaded and – as might well be expected – a naturally aristocratic young man of great charm. At the time I thought he was something of a dilettante because of his casual manner, but it was a misjudgement. He must have buckled down to work because he eventually got a master's degree and became a chartered accountant. Charles frequently went on weekend shoots to his home, Euston Hall, near Thetford in Norfolk.

Lord Ipswich was one of the group with Charles on this particular evening. As he came out of the club he recognized some friends in a car parked in the roadway. He trotted over, hammered on the roof of the car and shouted cheerfully, 'Come out, come out, whoever you are!'

The occupants didn't need a second invitation. Instead of being some of his aristocratic pals they were a group of Cambridge's choicest tearaways, nasty football hooligans in the making. Voices were raised, pushing quickly threatened to became flying fists... And Charles, loyal to his friend, showed he had as much physical courage as the moral courage he displayed at Gordonstoun. He wanted to help to take on the locals. But I hauled him away from the brawl as fast as I could and steered him back towards Trinity.

His blood was up, and he was furious with me that night for stopping him helping his friend. By next morning he had cooled down and accepted that perhaps I was right after all. We simply couldn't risk that sort of story breaking. In any case, by keeping Charles from wading in I took much of the steam out of the situation and there were no black eyes or bloody noses. Maybe Prince Philip wouldn't have been all that displeased to learn of his son's fighting to back up a friend, but I shudder to think how the Queen would have taken the news. Definitely not amused.

Trouble of the second kind – being the victim of others' machinations – arose while Charles was at Trinity.

At Cambridge, it was really difficult to guard him outside the college. For that matter things could be just as sticky inside, as I had discovered during another incident involving a very seductive-looking blonde, of whom more later.

When Charles cycled around Cambridge like most of the other undergraduates I didn't want to embarrass him or highlight his uniqueness by sticking close beside or just behind him like a police dog. I followed in the Land Rover at a reasonable distance, not to make it obvious that he was being shadowed by a protector and to preserve some sort of pretence that he was just an ordinary young man out on his own.

I was always uneasy and very much on the alert on these occasions, particularly when Charles became old enough to interest young women, and be interested in them. The opportunities for women to involve him in an 'incident' were all too many. The worst times were Rag Weeks, when licence became almost anarchy. The Manchester University

Rag Week of 1968 came within a hairsbreadth of being just that.

I learned 'through information received', as the timeworn police jargon goes, that a group of Manchester University women students, all Women's Libbers of the most strident kind, planned to raid Trinity, kidnap Charles and hold him to ransom. Usually there is a sort of friendly rivalry between universities, but this time there was a fifth column inside Cambridge. The would-be kidnappers from Manchester had found willing accomplices among the women of Girton College, Cambridge. The Women's Libbers were determined to pull off the coup without any male assistance whatsoever.

It was a well-planned operation almost worthy of professional kidnappers. They had hired a getaway car and arranged a hideaway for their prisoner. The actual snatch was going to be done by a squad of Amazons who, by all accounts, were built on the lines of Russian women shot-putters. These women were prepared to cart Prince Charles off bodily, and I'm certain they could have done it without breaking into a sweat.

I had the sneaking suspicion that Charles might even have enjoyed his captivity. However, as I was painfully aware that it would be my head that rolled into the basket, I was totally unamused.

I had a long and tough, unequivocal talk with one of the leaders of the would-be kidnappers, a slight, lissom and attractive young woman. I told her that we had all the details of the plan, and so it would inevitably fail, causing a great deal of trouble and pain to the women concerned. 'And,' I added, 'if you do go ahead and try to pull it off, I'll personally see that you won't want to sit down for a fortnight.'

Not the most brilliant of remarks, but it made my point.

She smiled at me, and replied softly. At first I couldn't believe my ears: she was calling me by all the four-letter names I'd ever heard, with a few more four-letter expletives thrown in for bad measure. This string of obscenities uttered in a Cheltenham accent sounded quite extraordinary, and I had second thoughts about whether Charles really would have secretly enjoyed being the women's prisoner. I don't know whether they would have scared him: but they certainly made me uneasy.

As a matter of fact this was not the first plot to kidnap Charles. Scotland Yard uncovered a plot by an Irish terrorist splinter group to kidnap him while he was at Cheam.

Charles didn't need third parties to get himself onto thin ice. Occasionally he galloped out onto it. There was an occasion when students decided to stage a sit-in at the Senate House in a protest against something or other. Charles decided he would join in with a couple of friends. I was appalled at the possible consequences, but for once Charles refused point-blank to do what I asked: stay away. I asked him what the motive was for the sit-in, why it was so important for him to take part, but he was rather vague about what the demonstration was meant to achieve. Then if it wasn't something he felt strongly about, why did he want to take part? I asked.

As far as I could make out from his answer Charles simply was curious to see what a sit-in was like, and – perhaps more importantly – he wanted to show his solidarity with his contemporaries. He was sure that there would be no personal danger to him – he was far from being physically afraid, but he was conscious of the necessary dignity of his position – and he was determined to show that he was a student like all the others. Which, as I have said before, he clearly wasn't.

I managed to win one concession from him. He agreed that he would go, if not in disguise, at least dressed inconspicuously and that he wouldn't draw attention to himself. 'How did you expect me to go ?' he asked in so many words. 'Wearing a crown?' He went into Trinity with his friends to change.

He might well have been less conspicuous in a crown. He and his friends – William Hastings-Bass, today a well-known racehorse trainer, was one of them – came out wearing trilby hats pulled down over their eyes and raincoats with the collars turned up. They stood out like three Al Capones at a Sunday School treat.

If that wasn't bad enough, Fate took an unkind hand. They were caught up in the crowd and swept into the very heart of the Senate House, where some of the more militant demonstrators had begun to shout at the police.

Away to one side I could see a press photographer battling his way through, camera at the ready.

With Prince Philip and Captain Iain Tennant, chairman of the Gordonstoun governors. The garden gateway was originally a fireplace in one of the Elgin Cathedral college houses, which were owned by the Gordonstoun estate.

December 1962, early morning: Prince Charles arrives at King's Cross after an overnight journey.

'If chance will have me king, why, chance may crown me.' Charles recreates Macbeth at Gordonstoun, 1966.

Unofficial photographs of Prince Charles were forbidden at Gordonstoun. This snap was on a film confiscated from a German visitor. Detective Chief Superintendent Perkins apparently did not recognize Prince Charles and said the film could be returned! Varney kept it.

Duncan, King of Scotland............. ....Barry Cooper
Malcolm...George Gordon
Donalbain...John Campbell
Macbeth..Prince Charles
Banquo..William Thomson
Macduff..Alastair Dobson
Lennox.....................................Nicholas Parry-Billings
Ross..Hamish Calder
Angus...Donald Coutts
Menteith...Brendon Bernard
Caithness....................................Alastair Fotheringham
Fleance, son to Banquo...........................Jeremy Bowen
Siward, general of the English forces.........Charles Hubbard
Young Siward, his son............................. Timothy Miles
Seyton, servant to Macbeth........ ....Andrew Lindsay
First Murderer..................................... David Finlayson
Second Murderer.. ....Malcolm Evans
Boy, son to Macduff..... .... Norman Illingworth
A Doctor ....William Shepherd
A Sergeant..James Joyce
A Porter...Philip Campbell
Lady Macbeth.................................Douglas Campbell
Lady Macduff..................................... Charles Fletcher
Gentlewoman................................ .Alexander Armitage
First Witch...Simon Lee
Second Witch...William Lloyd
Third Witch.... ....David Faber
Messengers, Soldiers and Attendants : Ian Adam-Cairns,
David Gerroll, Frederick Ditmas, John Brooke, James Muir,
Michael Collie.

Two cast lists from school drama days, taken from the original programmes. Top, as Macbeth, and below – playing a minor role this time – as the Duke of Exeter in *Henry the Fifth*.

 # The English

Chorus -- Jeremy Tulk-Hart
King Henry the Fifth................................David MacLehose
Archbishop of Canterbury.............................Patrick Ainley
Bishop of Ely..Barry Cooper
Duke of Exeter..Prince Charles
John, Duke of Bedford ....David Finlayson
Humphrey, Duke of Gloucester..........................James Joyce
Duke of York ....Andrew Michel
Earl of Salisbury...Timothy Lloyd
Earl of Westmorland ....David Brereton
Sir Thomas Erpingham ....John Bond
Captain Gower.......................................Michael Fabianski
Captain Fluellen.....................................Graham Burcher
Williams..Robin Tait
Bates ....Andrew Lindsay
Court...Philip Plumbe
Ancient Pistol..David Gwillim
Lieutenant Bardolph ....John Stonborough
Corporal Nym...Graham King
Mistress Quickly, the Hostess..........................Brian Fillery
Boy...John MacLeod

Scene : England and France

Time : 1415 - 1420

There will be one interval of ten minutes.

You are requested not to take photographs during the performance.

The first step on the Long, Slow Road to Buckingham Palace. Michael Varney's first day in uniform as a police cadet.

Prince Charles playing his part in rehearsals for one of the college revues at Cambridge.

Charles delivers a punnish monologue as a weather forecaster in 'Quiet Flows the Don', a revue staged by the Dryden Society, Trinity College.

Linda Berry ... Marylyn Muller
invite
H.R.H. The Prince of Wales
to a
PYJAMA PARTY
21st. Oct. at an Trempington Cellars
Hanerton from 8 p.m.
Please bring bottle + invitation.

'Please bring bottle and invitation.': Charles was forced to bow out of some of the college social whirl.

With Cambridge students on an archaeological dig in Jersey, 1968.

The quad at Trinity College.

Charles's room and the entrance to the E6 staircase, known as the 'Welsh Staircase' (both indicated).

Prince Charles with a Mr Lucas at the Cambridge University Polo Club practice ground, Woolmers Park.

Prince Charles at polo practice in Woolmers Park.

I dived into the mêlée. With me at this demonstration was Inspector Frank Cox of Cambridgeshire Special Branch. By sheer physical force, boosted by a charge of adrenalin set off by a mounting sense of panic, we managed to move Charles and his friends out of the line of fire. Seconds later the photographer's flashgun fired a fusillade. That was the slim margin by which 'militant' Charles avoided starring on Page One.

It was not as if the risk were for some passionately held belief. Later Charles admitted that he also found this demonstration uninspiring and pointless. He told me he thought that a lot of that sort of thing was to make changes simply for the sake of change. He was – and still is, according to some of his recent remarks about architecture – a traditionalist. Well, he *is* heir to the throne.

Potentially less explosive but amusing was his visit to the Rex Cinema with another two friends. As we arrived outside the cinema I saw that it was an adults-only, members-only cinema club. Although the film showing was innocuous enough, the Marx Brothers' *Duck Soup*, our way in was barred by the manager.

'All over twenty-one?' he asked.

'Yes,' I said, thus relieving Charles and his companions of the necessity of a direct lie. The manager handed over membership application forms. I passed on two of them but kept Charles's to myself. I feared that in his present state of embarrassment he would be quite capable of signing himself 'Prince Charles' – or just 'Charles', which would have provoked just as much comment. In those days I could often visualize newspaper headlines, and 'Prince Charles in Secret Adult Cinema Visit'...or even 'Secret VICE Cinema' would not be beyond certain papers.

I handed in the forms, and we went in.

'What name did you sign for me ?' he asked quietly.

'Well, the film's *Duck Soup*, so I signed "P. Green".'

He liked that.

There was another really major incident, engineered by others, which, without exaggeration, would have made the front page with centre-page spreads of all the 'popular' papers of the world.

One warm May morning in 1968 Charles gave me the keys

to his rooms and asked me to sort out for him certain books he would need for his next lecture. I entered his rooms, then stopped dead, unable to believe my eyes. Lying on his bed was a large, buxom blonde. She had a sleepy, slightly alcoholic smile on her face; but the main thing I noticed about her was the silver chain round her neck. The reason was, it was the only thing she was wearing.

The first thought that immediately flashed into my mind – well, the second thing, actually – was that I had heard that Ray Bellisario, the specialist in candid photographs of the royal family, was in the vicinity. And Charles was due back in his rooms from a tutorial at any moment. I could visualize only too vividly a three-sided collision between Charles, the naked blonde and Bellisario's camera. The world-wide headlines, stories and pictures were all too easy to imagine.

Somehow I just *had* to get the young woman out of the place and out of sight.

The first problem was, her clothes were nowhere to be seen, and I could think of no way I could smuggle a large, naked and probably completely helpless blonde out of the place in broad daylight. I rushed around and eventually found them hidden behind some books in the study. I grabbed them and thrust them at her. She smiled up at me, rolled over and fell asleep again.

There was no time for niceties of behaviour. I somehow dragged her to a sitting position, and then onto her feet. Maybe it was only to help herself stand upright that she wrapped her arms round my neck. 'I like you,' she said. 'Do you like me ?' and she breathed the equivalent of two dry Martinis into my face. There were footsteps in the corridor and my heart thumped in my chest, but they went on past.

As I slipped one of her feet into her knickers we swayed, then staggered across the floor like a couple of inept adagio dancers before crashing into the furniture. We rebounded onto the bed. She was giggling helplessly, but I was monumentally unamused. Apart from anything else I was worried that someone might hear the girlish giggles and the creaking bed and come to all the wrong conclusions both about what was going on and who it was going on with.

I managed to free myself and stood up. Since that day I have always admired undertakers for being able to dress bodies. I had never tried to dress a horizontal, unco-operative girl before that moment, and I have never tried again. Somehow I got her into her skirt, sweater and shoes. I tucked her tights and bra in my pocket, heaved her upright again and took her to the door. I peered out into the corridor. There was no sign of Bellisario, or, God be thanked, anyone else.

With my arm round her we slid and staggered down the staircase and across New Court to the comparative safety of my own rooms. Fortunately the gods that take care of drunks, and of the people that take of the drunks, were feeling kind: there were not too many people about. Perhaps a few of them were slightly envious to see me with an attractive young blonde who'd managed to make me perspire profusely, but most of them were too polite – or preoccupied – to pay much attention.

After a great deal of hot black coffee internally and cold water externally she began to tell me as much as she knew of the story. The rest of the details I managed to dig out later from other sources until I had a full picture.

For once I had done Bellisario an injustice: he had nothing to do with the set-up – probably only because he hadn't thought of the idea. Certainly he would have taken full advantage of the situation if he had known about it.

The whole thing started as a typical college prank, if any one of them can be called 'typical'. Someone suggested that it would be a real hoot to plant a woman in Charles's bed. The blonde had won an anonymous vote for the role, and it wasn't difficult to see why. She was built on most generous lines, and had a character to match.

Apparently the jokers 'borrowed' Charles's room key from his pocket while he was playing squash one day, and had a copy cut. The young woman herself had no idea of the part she was going to play. On the night chosen for the performance, she was warmed up with a bucketful of large gins at an all-night party. During the next morning she was escorted to Charles's room and stripped by the other women taking part in the 'joke'. At least, that was the theory. Just to make sure she stayed – although in her condition she was unlikely to get up from the bed – they hid her clothes. God knows what I should have done if the others had taken her clothes with them!

On this occasion I was able to keep the incident more or less secret. I did it not at all for the students' sake and not principally for the blonde's. My main concern was, as always, Prince Charles. I never forgot the furore that was provoked by the cherry brandy incident. Charles was the natural target for jokers and for sensation-mongers. But once again I managed to keep him out of the headlines despite a very narrow squeak. For the most part he was aware of his own vulnerablity as far as the press was concerned, but just once in a while he walked into situations that made my blood run cold, like this one.

The events weren't always deadly serious and fraught, though. Apart from being the object of practical jokes of dubious humour, Charles was the target for some quite extraordinary postal pornography...although he never saw it. At Trinity I collected his mail from the porter's lodge, and if there were any strange-looking packets or letters I checked them before passing them on. Personal letters from people who knew Charles could always be recognized by a simple code in the address and they always went direct to him.

In what might be described as 'unsolicited correspondence' there was always the very remote possibility of a bomb, and the very real possibility of hard pornography and obscenity. This latter category came from both women and men, and the letters all had one thing in common: they described in some detail exactly what the writer would like to do with or to Charles. I was surprised – at first, anyway – that some of the letters were obviously written by people of some education and background.

The most remarkable correspondence came in an envelope with the well-known acronym SWALK – 'sealed with a loving kiss' – written across it. Not the sort of thing one would expect from a hard-porn enthusiast. It seemed harmless enough.

The envelope contained a section of a photograph accompanied by a short letter. The picture was of a woman's bare midriff; the letter contained a promise of photographs of more parts of her anatomy in future correspondence, and an uninhibited account of how the girl would make love to Charles – given the opportunity, of course. It was all very advanced stuff: definitely post-graduate.

Further letters continued to arrive, each containing a photograph of another part of female anatomy and a letter on the same theme as before. These letters were all delivered by hand, and at a time when the porter's lodge was temporarily deserted. I spent as much time as I possibly could keeping the lodge under observation, but I never saw the woman. It shouldn't have been difficult to spot her, even though none of the pictures was of her face. The rest of her, judging from the pieces of photograph I had managed to put together, must have been spectacular, even fully clothed. I was badly piqued that I couldn't catch her, and for two reasons: professional pride and sheer curiosity to see the exciting-looking young woman.

One day I was walking into the hall with the porter when an elderly man, who would have been perfect casting for a senior professor in a film, met us on the way out. He saw me, half-checked and then hurried past, eyes averted.

I ran the last few yards to the lodge, and there on the counter was another SWALK letter. I dashed outside again, but the elderly man had disappeared.

I never saw him again, and there were no more letters.

There was another regular delivery for Charles. An anonymous joker took out a subscription to Playboy in the Prince's name. Of course, in those days it was a very much more innocuous publication – pictorially, anyway. The day after it was delivered to him Charles would hand it to me with a smile and a remark like, 'More in your line, Varney.'

Well, I was nine years older.

And I was enough of a detective to see that the magazine had been well looked at before it came to me.

10   The Play's the Thing (Again) – and Girls

Charles was always a doer and enjoyed practical things. There was his cello, of course, and although it could be a fairly static activity, there was fishing. He painted a little and some of his work decorated – if that is the word – the walls of one of the Sandringham estate homes. He took up flying, played polo and went sailing. All this, while studying for a degree and fulfilling outside engagements.

Sometimes when I studied his daily timetable I was reminded of an old joke about a farmer's wife in pre-TV days who was being interviewed by a Ministry of Agriculture and Fisheries researcher. She explained that she got up at 5.30 to milk the cows, then got the farmworkers' breakfasts. After that she did housework in the farmhouse. Next job was preparing the men's midday meal, cooking and serving it, and in the afternoon she worked in the dairy. After that she made bread and prepared the evening meal, and when that was done she set into jam-making or preparing potted meat or making sausages. Of course, twice a week she went to market and did the shopping.

The Ministry man finally asked her what she did in her spare time. The farmer's wife thought for a long moment and said, 'I go to the lavatory.'

Gordonstoun had instilled in Charles the importance of physical fitness: he was always careful of what he ate and was keen on exercise. His excellent condition enabled him to do more than the average student without tiring.

There were times when I found it hard to keep up with him. My hours were long – in fact, I was on call twenty-four hours a day, although in practice I did get time to myself while he was safely in the Wren Library, or at Prince Richard's house for example. But Charles packed his days with activity.

Soon after the Prince arrived at Trinity I decided that it would be a good thing if I took a first-aid course. I'd been given the basic first-aid training when I first became a policeman, but I'd become rather rusty; and in any case, I wanted to be able to cope with something more complicated than a cut finger if Charles should have an accident while I was with him. Rather more practically, first aid was one of the subjects I had to pass as part of my promotion examinations. Arrangements were made for me to attend lectures with the Cambridge Police Force, part of the Mid-Anglia Constabulary.

Charles had an enquiring mind and was always ready to learn something new. When I told him I was taking the course he showed a keen interest in the subject, and after a while attended the lectures with me. I quietly wondered how many young women would have had a fit of the vapours and swooned at his feet if they'd known that he was skilled in mouth-to-mouth resuscitation. Or that one of the first essentials of dealing with someone who has fainted is to loosen all tight clothing.

While he was at Gordonstoun he became interested in pottery and showed some pieces in the school's exhibition of work. At Cambridge he somehow found time to take it up again for a while. He went to evening classes at the Cambridgeshire College of Arts and Technology, which catered for full- and part-time students. There were fourteen or fifteen students in the class. Some were locals, others came from St Ives, Bury St Edmunds, Littleport and Alconbury. Charles's presence in a class inevitably did a lot for recruitment.

He was introduced to the course by the wife of Dr Bevan, his physician. Mrs Bevan was a charming lady, and frequently Charles (and I) visited the Bevan home after classes when Dr and Mrs Bevan and Charles would discuss their work. My contribution to the discussion was a discreet silence. My lack of appreciation of pottery came a close second to music.

Charles's interest in the pottery course evaporated fairly quickly. One of the factors that accelerated the process was probably that although there were some men students in his class they were heavily outnumbered by married women. The major cause, however, was his increasing interest in acting, his favourite public activity.

At Cambridge Charles was keen to get back on the stage, but he was uncertain how Lord Butler would react to the idea. In fact the Master encouraged him to join the Dryden Society, Trinity College's amateur dramatic society. I was rather surprised when Charles told me, but he went on to say that Butler had considered that more experience on the stage would help prepare him for public occasions, and for television appearances in particular. Butler, of course, knew of Charles's success in *Macbeth* at Gordonstoun, and presumably expected him to carry on along those lines. He probably knew, too, that Charles was a firmly religious and conservatively moral young man, who never used really bad language, so he was unlikely to appear in anything outrageous. But what Butler probably did not know was that the Prince had a great love of practical joking, of saucy student humour. He was about to indulge these fancies publicly.

At the beginning of his second year at Cambridge Charles auditioned for a part in the college's next production, which called for him to mime, improvise and deliver a prepared speech. The audition earned him a role...as the parson in *Erpingham Camp* by the already notorious Joe Orton. As if that wasn't far enough removed from *Macbeth*, he had a custard pie pushed in his face and the part called for him to be pelted with pork pies. It was the sort of performance that might have prepared a future politician for public appearances, but not, I'd hope, the heir to the throne.

Three months later Charles was on the stage once more, this time in a show that was even farther from classical theatre: a revue called *Revulution*. As soon as it was known that the Prince would appear in a public performance there was a thriving black market in the 4s. (20 pence) tickets –

even in a couple of foreign capitals!

When I saw the show, so accustomed was I to being with a rather quiet, introverted Prince Charles that some of the lines made my jaw drop. There was nothing really objectionable, but the stage revue-artiste Charles was so unlike the serious, slightly shy student I was used to being with.

As he walked off stage, leering at a pretty girl, he told the audience, 'I like giving myself heirs…' Which was very funny. In another sketch he played a pop-star cellist who had just been released from prison after serving a sentence for smoking chicory. The pop-star was described as 'the biggest plucker in the business'.

He sent himself up gently when he played a singing dustman, an allusion to an article he had written in Varsity complaining that the banging-about of dustbins and dustman Frank Clarke's singing woke him too early in the morning. As a result of the incident Clarke briefly became a minor celebrity when he sang on TV. In the revue Charles sat in a dustbin on stage while he was being interviewed by the Press, and asked 'What about me £5?'

A funny line with a fairly obvious point seen by the entire audience also had an underlying very private allusion which meant something only to Charles and me. On the stage he raised an umbrella and remarked 'I lead a very sheltered life.' As soon as I heard the words my memory flashed back to an incident a couple of years or so previously.

I was driving back to Buckingham Palace with the young Princess Anne and Charles after a *son et lumière* display at St Paul's Cathedral. As we made our way back through the late-night traffic we noticed a young couple kissing on the edge of the pavement, heedless to the rest of the world.

'I wish we didn't live such sheltered lives,' Anne said wistfully. 'Don't you?' she asked her brother.

He rounded on her immediately. 'You mustn't ever say that. I know it's true, but you mustn't ever say it.'

'*I lead a very sheltered life,*' Charles said, making a joke of it. It was something I've always liked and admired about him: his ability to laugh at himself; but I'm sure that he had a twinge of secret regret when he spoke his line.

It wasn't until a great deal later that I realized that I, too, had led a very sheltered life during the time I was Charles's detective. I had missed a great deal of a life that I had previously taken for granted, and the effect was severe. But more of that later.

His next revue – and practically his last stage appearance – was *Quiet Flows the Don* in which he almost put on a one-man show: he appeared in twenty-five of the thirty sketches. He was kept as busy as a one-armed paperhanger in a high wind. The material was much the same as before, with perhaps a stronger element of sexual suggestiveness. As a BBC weather forecaster he announced: 'It is 06.00 hours. Virility at first will be poor. Promiscuity will be widespread....Listeners are advised to avoid falling barometers and on funday and boozeday there will be bold and rowdy conditions...'

It was clear that Charles hugely enjoyed his stage appearances. 'It's great fun,' he told me. 'I love doing it.' Later he added, more significantly, 'It helps to keep me sane.'

He entered whole-heartedly into the general hilarity and mildly risqué jokes in *Erpingham Camp* and his various revue appearances. The Charles on the stage was a different and separate man from the moral and religious Prince Charles, heir to the throne.

As an aside, I had my own small connection with the stage. Apart from appearing with a local repertory company with Ralph Lynn in *Witness for the Prosecution* when I was stationed at Hunstanton in 1958-9, I briefly ran the Alan Russell Theatrical Agency in Charing Cross Road, which belonged to friends, Helen and Arthur Loman. To give them a chance to take a break I sat in for them during a spell of accumulated leave.

At a lunch with Arthur, Lionel Gamlin of *British Movietone News* and the distinguished actor Michael Gwynn at the Green Room Club in John Adam Street, Lionel assumed that I was full-time in showbiz. He asked me what I was doing at the moment.

'I'm with the student prince at Cambridge,' I told him.

'Good God!' said Lionel. 'They're not reviving that old thing again!'

When I first became a royal protection officer I became aware that for all the royal family's privileges many small pleasures we take for granted are denied them. At Cambridge there was one more that Charles had to forego. When he was with a girl – or more precisely, young woman – in public he could make no gesture of simple friendship such as putting an arm round her. The gesture would inevitably be misinterpreted, exaggerated and made the fertile ground of enormous speculation. This situation made anything more than a casual acquaintanceship with a woman difficult. It imposed on him a necessity to be very careful in his selection of real girlfriends. Self-promoters and even mildly irresponsible women had to be carefully avoided. There was an intense newspaper and public interest in what should have been his private life. A transitory minor indiscretion by a girlfriend of the Prince of Wales could easily become a long-running major story. Fortunately he was able to enjoy women's company in private places away from public observation.

Charles's first close woman friend at Cambridge was Lucia Santa Cruz, the daughter of a Chilean diplomat. She had a great deal to commend her. As the daughter of an ambassador she was accustomed to moving in the upper levels of society. She might be impressed by a Prince of Wales, but she was not overwhelmed by him.

Lucia Santa Cruz was sophisticated and – a great advantage for a young man's first serious woman friend – she was four years older than Charles. She was a PhD, at Cambridge because she was doing research for Lord Butler for his autobiography. All these are formidable qualifications, but she was also a strikingly good-looking young woman.

Theoreticlly, conditions at Trinity were not favourable for a serious romance because there was a night-time curfew at the college and the gate was locked. Fortunately for Charles, Lord Butler was opposed to this curfew rule. He readily gave Lucia a key to the Master's Lodge when Charles asked if she might stay there for privacy, and the Prince had his own key, of course.

As far as I could tell the relationship was a typical 'first-love' infatuation, and Charles was aware that it could never come to anything because Lucia was a Catholic. She gave him an invaluable gift: the first seeds of self-confidence with women. Afterwards he had a string of steady girlfriends, almost all of them well connected socially if not fully paid-up members of the aristocracy.

Another attractive young woman who became a very close friend of Charles at Cambridge was Sybilla Dorman, daughter of the then Governor of Malta, who was reading history at Newnham. Whether she really enjoyed slaughtering birds or not she would often join Charles on a weekend shoot at Wood Farm on the Sandringham estate. I used arrange to have the pheasants she shot plucked and dressed. She went to a couple of cocktail parties at Buckingham Palace with him, which aroused a lot of speculation among the professional and amateur Charles-watchers, who started trying to marry him off even while he was still at university. On several occasions he also had dinner in her rooms in Newnham College – I suppose she cooked him the pheasants I had prepared for her; – and they had a holiday together in Malta. Cindy Buxton, whom I mention later, was among Charles's girlfriends. She, too, was able to see Charles away from the public eye because he used to go shooting on her father's estate.

These were girlfriends, even the more senior Lucia Santa Cruz, but he had a lady friend, too. I call her that because she was rather older than the others: an Australian named Angela, who lived in Chelsea. The strong impression I got of this relationship was that more than anything else Charles turned to her for companionship and advice – the sort of advice he couldn't get from another man.

For the rest of the time I was his protection officer, Charles was never without a 'steady'. Yet despite this newfound pleasure of close relationships with women, despite the calls on his time by his interest in acting, by his semi-official and official visits, by his shooting and polo, he worked hard at his studies.

As I have said elsewhere, there weren't many things I envied Charles, but his effortless success with women was definitely one of them. He didn't have to go out of his way to make their acquaintance; on the contrary, he had to duck a lot of advances that were directed at him. Some of them were so wildly aimed that they hit innocent bystanders. On reflection, perhaps some of the advances weren't so badly aimed, and some of the bystanders weren't all that innocent.

Women were always something of a trial to Prince Charles. I don't mean that he had any bother in finding girlfriends: quite the contrary. The difficulty was avoiding them. Not all of them, of course... But the problems with women spilled over onto those close to him – including myself. There were two incidents in particular which affected me quite deeply. I recount them here because they have a particular relevance to Prince Charles's life at Cambridge and to his character.

The first involved a strikingly beautiful woman of about forty, well known in society. She often figured in photographs of parties printed in the *Tatler*, and she was referred to respectfully in gossip columns. I shall call her 'Lady Helen', although that was neither her name or her rank.

I met Lady Helen in the Coach and Horses in Trumpington, not far from the Gog Magog Hills to the south-east of Cambridge. I was keeping a discreet eye on Charles, who was having lunch with Squadron Leader Checketts. As usual, I had found a place in a corner with my back to the wall where I could keep the whole room under observation without appearing to. The restaurant was crowded, and Lady Helen came to where I was sitting and asked if she might share my table. It would have been churlish – and pointless – to refuse, and in any case she reminded me that she had been at a party with Charles and me a few nights earlier. As she sat down I looked across her shoulder at Charles, who raised his eyebrows in approval.

Lady Helen and I exchanged some small – very small -talk for a while. (Going to parties with Charles and constantly inadvertently overhearing his chat with his friends, I had learnt a little of the art of inconsequential conversation.) She was taking an interest in my work as Charles's detective, but not enough to set any alarm bells ringing in my head, and then she asked whether I was literally on duty seven days and nights a week. I told her that occasionally, when Charles attended a private function in a secure place, I was able to have a couple of hours to myself. Like, I added, the following night, when he was going to a private dinner party.

'Then why don't you slip over to our place for a while?' Lady Helen asked. 'We're having a few friends over for drinks and I know my husband would love to meet you.' I thought she was overstating her husband's probable reaction, but he could well be mildly curious to meet the man who was always close to Prince Charles and responsible for his safety. People usually were, but I told them little enough, and nothing about his private life.

The following evening I delivered Charles safely to No.1 Victoria Street, Prince Richard's Cambridge home, and arranged to pick him up about four hours later. I was rather more nattily dressed than usual, but Charles didn't seem to notice, or if he did, he made no comment. Then I set off for my own evening out.

Lady Helen and her husband lived out in the country in a handsome house in its own grounds. As I pulled up by the front door I subconsciously felt there was something slightly odd. But, quite frankly, I was so looking forward to seeing Lady Helen again that it didn't occur to me until I was inside the house and it was too late anyway. To my surprise Lady Helen herself opened the door to me, and I had an awful feeling that I'd arrived too early, because she was informally dressed in an attractive housecoat. It was then that I realized what it was that had seemed odd to me when I arrived. There were no other cars parked by the house.

Lady Helen explained that her husband had been suddenly called away on business and they'd had to put off the party. She would have informed me but didn't know how to get into touch with me. Still, now I was there, the least she could do was offer me a drink.

She was chatty and friendly, and we got on very well together. My years with Charles made me perfectly at ease there, despite the fact that before I became his protection officer I should have been allowed in that house only by the servants' entrance. When I began to get the feeling that she was sending out sexual signals I dismissed the idea as being wishful thinking, but soon they became quite clear. And then she said, 'I knew right away that you and I could be friends. I wonder if I know you well enough to ask a favour? My daughter so wants to meet Prince Charles...'

My spirits fell. So that's what it was all about. I promised to introduce them at the very next party.

To my surprise, instead of starting to show me out now she had got what she wanted Lady Helen became even more intimate.

'Look, why not bring Prince Charles over here for a weekend?' she asked. 'I want my daughter and Charles to become friends. Very good, close friends. And if you can help me, you'll find I can be very generous.'

I was thoroughly fed up by now, and I flatly told her that I couldn't just ask Charles away for a weekend somewhere.

'Oh, I know you can do it. I'm told that Prince Charles trusts you.'

'Which was the very reason I can't – won't – help you.'

In the words of the famous cliché, I made an excuse and left. But before I got to the door she took me by the arm and pulled me close. 'Don't come to a hasty decision.' And as I walked away she added, 'Remember, I can be very generous.'

I clashed the gears badly twice as I drove away from the house, half in anger at myself for having been taken in and half in disappointment. I had an almost overwhelming urge to turn back again. As I drove back to Cambridge I hoped that no one would tempt me like that again; but I was fairly sure that in Cambridge, with Charles, there would be other temptations. I was right: there were, but none as powerful as Lady Helen. No, not quite none...

From the moment at Gordonstoun when Charles and his friends started giving girls marks out of ten, I heard him give ten marks only twice. The first was a young woman we passed on the street and never saw again. She was a Swedish type: blonde, full-bodied and heavily tanned with shoulder-length hair. She was laughing, and I think that earned her the tenth mark, for Charles liked girls who laughed. From what I had seen and heard of Charles, she was very much his type.

The second girl to score the very rare ten was the daughter of someone prominent in racing circles. I shall call her 'Penny'.

I met Penny at a party I attended with Charles. I say that I met her, because that is what happened. Charles was there, but I actually met her and spoke to her; he did not. At most of the parties I went to with Charles I was hardly of the same social standing as the majority of the guests. So, although I had become comfortable at being in the background of his background, as it were, I took good care not to become too intimate with any of his friends or acquaintances. In fact, paradoxically, I had a much closer relationship with Charles himself, even though he was a good few rungs on the social ladder above the other people at the parties. I knew him and had been by his side during his most unguarded moments for some years.

But to return to Penny. When we first started talking, I was fairly wary of her. In the past many attractive young women had chatted me up, but I was very conscious that they were doing it not because of my irresistible charm, but, as I have said, because they could see in me an easy way to be introduced to Prince Charles. The Lady Helen incident had also left its mark on me.

Penny, though, was completely different from all the other young women taking part in the Royal Hunt of the Prince.

In a sentence, I fell in love with her, physically and spiritually.

The fact that I couldn't give her all the things that she had been used to didn't trouble her at all. Indeed, I realized later that she already *had* everything. Her father was well-to-do and thoroughly spoiled her with money and material things. Nevertheless, she was not as selfish as she might well have become. She could be kind, and she had compassion. But Penny wanted the best of everything, and was given it. Even Nature had been generous in with gifts of a lovely face and a beautiful body. We began to see each other frequently, and suddenly, for me it was a very serious thing.

Before one Saturday night party she asked me if I would introduce her to Charles. I was as proud of being with her as an Olympic gold-medal winner, and I was delighted to be able to show her off to Prince Charles. I agreed to introduce her.

'Is that a promise?' she asked.

I nodded, and she didn't mention the subject again. It was another example of how she was different from the other women, who constantly pestered for introductions.

I knew that Charles had shown a great deal of interest in Penny. There were times when he seemed unable to take his eyes off her – and no wonder. She could have been designed to his personal specifications, like the Swedish girl who'd deserved the ten out of ten.

I introduced them and Charles stayed chatting rather

longer than he usually did. He was friendly and charming to her and said he hoped they'd meet again.

'I hope so, too,' she said demurely.

Charles paused and then winked at me. 'Come to think of it, I'm sure we will,' he told her.

As I said, I knew Charles extremely well by this time, and I was aware that what he meant was that he and Penny were bound to meet because she had become a feature of my life. But she – not unreasonably, really – interpreted his remark in an entirely different way.

What she did not know was that Charles didn't make overt passes at women in public, and absolutely never at women who were with his friends.

That night, on the way home to Trinity, he said with a heavy casualness that made me slightly uneasy, 'Quite a girl!'

'Ten out of ten?' I suggested.

He nodded in agreement.

The following day Penny turned up unexpectedly at my rooms. There was something strangely secretive about her manner. She was wearing a white mink coat, and I asked her if there was some special occasion.

'Sort of,' she said, and asked for a drink.

Again, in a sentence, she made it clear to me that she had come to my rooms to go to bed with me.

'There's one thing you have to understand,' she said as she began to undress. 'This is the first and the last time.' I didn't answer her, so she went on. 'You did me a favour last night, and I always pay my debts.'

The message was clear enough, even for a totally infatuated idiot like me. She had been much cleverer than the other women who had tried to use me to get an introduction to Charles. She had charmed me expertly and overcome my normal caution: she had fooled me completely. I'd served my purpose, and now I was going to be paid off.

I managed to say 'Put your clothes on and get out of here, or I'll put you out the way you are.'

Penny quickly dressed again. Halfway to the door she paused and said, 'I didn't handle that very well, did I? I'm sorry.'

I felt quite awful. I tried to tell myself that you can't lose something you never had in the first place. But I *thought* I had it, and the sense of loss was just as keen.

The point of this story is not my lack of perception or my unhappy experience at the hands of ambitious women but to show to what lengths women would go to for a chance to get close to Charles. Yet supposing that Penny *had* succeeded in marrying Charles. How would a future Queen feel, remembering that she had slept with someone just to get an introduction to Charles? And Lady Helen: how would a king's mother-in-law live with the memory that she had gone to bed with his detective just for an opportunity to thrust her daughter at the Prince?

I suppose the women's ambition was so intense that they could think of nothing else, neither of their own dignity nor of how it could leave them open to gossip.

The incidents also brought home to me the temptations that must have been put in Charles's path. If the Prince's detective could get offers like these, what on earth must he have been subjected to! He did marvellously well not to get involved in any public scandals.

There was a further lesson to be drawn from these adventures. I realized that Charles's instincts and perceptions were acute. Penny probably thought that I had told him the whole story, but I didn't. Charles was shrewd enough to guess that the ten-out-of-ten beauty was also a determined schemer. Although Penny and I never went out together again we did see each other at a couple of parties, but Charles had nothing to do with her. Nor did Lady Helen and her daughter ever get a second look. His instincts were very strong. He had girlfriends, but he didn't pick any wrong 'uns.

11 Out and About

Charles was an *enthusiastic* driver, I suppose the word is. It was all a part of his complex character that although he was reserved or timid or even shy with people when he was young, this did not mean he lacked physical courage. In adult life after he left Cambridge his confidence with complicated machinery like helicopters, aircraft and naval ships was well demonstrated. So, when he was up at Trinity he was never scared or nervous behind the wheel of a car. The same could not be said of his passengers.

Cambridge undergraduates were not allowed to drive cars in their first year. Thereafter they were forbidden to drive them within the city limits, otherwise the town's already crowded roads would have been choked with old bangers. When Charles wanted to go out in his own car, to Sandringham at a weekend, for example, I used to drive him to the outskirts of the town in the Land Rover to where his blue MGC (*not* an MGB, as has often been stated) was garaged. From there on he would take over and drive us to our destination.

Despite some of the rather hairy and odd trips I made in that car – or maybe because of them – I remember it with a great deal of affection. The car was a fairly rare model: not many of them were made, and it is now in the museum at Sandringham. It had a marvellous bullhorn fitted – a present, I think, from Prince Richard. Certainly Richard demonstrated the magnificent instrument on a journey from Fochabers to Balmoral. The two young Princes had a great time with it. One blast of the horn and cows came charging across the fields towards them.

Lord Butler, the Master, was always amused to see us set off in the Land Rover, Charles sitting innocently beside me. He once told the Prince he wasn't being fooled: Butler knew very well what Charles was up to. Whatever other walks of life in which Charles might have been successful, being a criminal was not one of them: his face dropped a yard and was better than a signed confession.

Although we had some fairly hairy moments in the MGC, it was in my own car that I had the most embarrassing incident with Charles. I was driving him to Mundford, near Thetford, for a fishing trip on the River Wissey, in my Vauxhall Cresta because the Land Rover was in for service. We left Cambridge rather late, and Charles was in a hurry to get to Mundford. He kept urging me to go faster, pulling my leg with remarks like, 'Have you got the handbrake on?' and 'Move over, Varney; there's a funeral trying to overtake.' I drove fairly fast, but well within my own limits, taking advantage of the straight A45 and the good visibility.

Charles was making another remark about the way I was dawdling along when I noticed a man in dark trousers and a light-coloured shirt bending over something on the nearside of the road.

'Any minute now a policeman's going to step out into the road and wave us down,' I said.

'Is this a joke, or do you have second sight?' Charles asked me.

'Neither,' I told him.

'So how do you know?'

'I think we've just been through a radar trap.'

I had hardly finished the sentence when a uniformed PC stepped out onto the road some distance ahead and signalled to us to stop.

I pulled up, got out and moved a few paces from the car in an attempt to avoid any general embarrassment.

'Good afternoon, officer,' I said politely. 'Is there a problem?'

The rest of the interview followed the lines I knew so well.

'Is this your car, sir?'

'Yes.'

'Can you tell me the registration number, please?'

'Yes. It's...' I checked, just before I gave him the number of my old car. 'It's...' I repeated, and stopped again. I couldn't remember the number of this new car. What I did remember, unfortunately, was that I hadn't notified the local police of its registration number. As I started to explain that I had only just bought the car, I knew I sounded as unconvincing as a swaying drunk trying to persuade a policeman that he'd had only one half pint at lunchtime. Nor had I got my insurance certificate with me, or any document to prove I did own the car.

Although I normally tried to avoid doing it, I had no alternative to getting out my warrant card and showing it to the officer. He was quite unimpressed. If anything, his disapproval became more evident. I'd forgotten how antipathetic some local police feel towards 'fellow-officers' from the Met.

'Look,' I said, making my local accent even more pronounced, 'I've got Prince Charles in the car, and we're late for an appointment; that's why I may have let the speed creep up without noticing it.'

I glanced round at the car. Charles was keeping his head down and trying to seem as anonymous as possible. He needn't have bothered. The constable didn't even trouble himself to look at him.

'Oh, yeah,' he replied. 'Fancy. Now, I shall report you for exceeding the speed limit. You are not obliged to say anything, but anything you do say –'

'Will be taken down in writing and may be used in evidence,' I finished for him.

As the constable gave me the slip of paper telling me that I had to produce my insurance certificate at a police station within seven days he muttered, 'Got Prince Charles in the car. Huh.'

As we drove off Charles leant forward and hid his face by pretending to blow his nose into a large handkerchief. The constable still wasn't looking.

This incident was only rather embarrassing. Charles's haste to get to his destination on another occasion was hair-raising. We were on our way from Cambridge to Petworth House for an overnight stay before playing polo.

On this occasion Charles drove the celebrated MGC GT because one of us had to map-read, and he rather craftily claimed that he wasn't very good at it. I should find our way rather better than he would, he claimed.

It was a miserable, wet night. We set off sedately enough, but once we were out of the town Charles began to put on speed. We'd already lost our way a couple of times before we got onto the A3, which, although it wasn't a double carriageway throughout its full length, was quite a fast road nevertheless. Charles, never a dawdling driver at the worst of times, took full advantage of it.

Like most of the royal family the Prince started driving before the legal age on the private roads of the Sandringham and Balmoral estates, where there was no traffic to contend with, and anyone on foot would take good care to get out of the way. Perhaps it gave him a false sense of security on public roads and encouraged him to whiz about a bit sometimes.

'Take it easy,' I said. 'We don't want to miss our turn-off.'

'Just tell me in good time,' Prince Charles replied, going a little faster.

'We take the next turning on the – …That's it!' I shouted; then, 'Don't stop!' There was a car close – too close – behind us. On the wet surface he would have run into the back of us. It would have been completely the other driver's fault, but I didn't want Charles to be involved in a traffic accident on a dark, wet night'

'Now what do we do?' Charles asked, glaring at the car as it overtook us.

'There's another turn-off just a bit further on. We can double back from there and pick up the other road.' I glanced at the map. 'It's about another mile.'

I kept a sharp lookout to give him warning in good time. Up ahead I could see the signpost and was just about to tell Charles when he pulled out into the outside lane to overtake another car. Maybe it was the one that had been close behind us at the last turn-off and had prevented him from braking sharply.

'Don't overtake!' I shouted. 'There's our turn-off!'

It was too late. He was committed to overtaking the other car, and roared past the road junction.

The fact that we were now running even later because of the two missed turn-offs made Charles still more agitated: he put his foot down harder.

We were rapidly becoming more and more lost as we raced in the wrong direction, away from our destination.

'Where do we go from here?' he asked sharply.

Trying to read a sheet map at night in a sports car with a folding roof is not the easiest of tasks even in the best of circumstances. When you're trying to keep one eye on the road and other traffic and not enjoying what you're seeing it becomes an almost impossible exercise. I managed to get a quick glance at Prince Charles. I could just see that he had that familiar determined, almost sulky look that has become well known from a thousand Press pictures.

'Look,' I called out against the sound of the rushing wind and noisy engine, 'if you don't stop or slow down we'll never find the way to Petworth. We're going right away from it now.'

'We'll go back, then,' he said shortly.

Before I could work out the best place to turn he shot down a small side road. He undertook a three-point turn of sorts. The trouble was, it involved *reversing* out onto and across part of the A3. At night.

The only explanation of how we got across without having a fearsome accident must be that God was on our side.

We drove back down the road at a more respectable speed. I was speechless as I weighed up just how far I dared go in commenting on that particular piece of driving. My first words were, 'Take the next turn-off on the right.' There must have been something in my tone of voice. Charles turned towards me and gave that famous big smile with a faint hint of apology about it. The charm was irresistible. I had to smile back. But it must have been a twitchy smile.

One way and another, long before he went into the Navy, I should think that Prince Charles heard more shots fired in anger than most professional soldiers who have not fought in a war. True, the shots were fired at pheasants, grouse and other game birds, some rabbits and a few stags; nevertheless, when following him around there were periods when I seemed to have a permanent smell of gunpowder in my nostrils.

(Incidentally, I have never understood how people active in the preservation of wildlife can find pleasure in killing birds: the often-advanced theory that game is 'preserved' by shooting hundreds of them is beyond me. As far as members of the royal family and their friends are concerned, they don't even have the excuse of killing for food.)

Sometimes it seemed that Cambridge was nothing more than an interlude between shoots at Wood Farm, the number of times we went there. One thing was for sure: Wood Farm was no place for a pheasant. The poor creatures were massacred with great enthusiasm and precision. (Prince Philip had a shrewd eye for the main chance: he had the birds marketed, sometimes for as much as £2 a brace. I think a local dealer in King's Lynn had a contract for selling all royal game.)

Wood Farm, an old stone house on the Sandringham estate, was originally known as Dr Ansell's House. Charles hadn't yet gone up to Cambridge when Dr Ansell retired, but it was seized on as a perfect place for the Prince to be able to get away from the inevitable increased publicity and attention that would result from his living in college. It could also be used for repaying hospitality on a scale that would clearly be impracticable at his rooms in college.

The house was long and narrow and constructed of a material that was very familiar to me, Norfolk rubble, which is a mixture of flint and stone; the roof was of red tiles. Near the entrance to the drive was another cottage which would serve for staff accommodation.

Although originally Wood Farm was primarily meant for Charles, everyone could see the advantage in having it open all the year round and not having to open up the main house on the estate. So the farmhouse itself was refurbished and a great deal of work done on the grounds before the place was ready for occupation by the royal family. Inside there were some paintings that would have fetched high prices at auction – not because they were particularly marvellous works of art but because the artists were Prince Philip and Prince Charles.

When Chief Superintendent Perkins first briefed me about weekends at Wood Farm he told me that the occasions would be informal – which was another way of saying that everyone staying there would pitch in at everything that needed doing. It was one of the few occasions when I thought that the Chief Superintendent had an unconscious sense of humour.

Nevertheless, there *were* times when there was a certain lack of ceremony and a temporary lowering of class-barriers. On one of my visits with Prince Charles the house party consisted of the Duke of Edinburgh, Admiral Christopher (soon afterwards Admiral Sir Christopher) Bonham-Carter, his wife and three other guests. They were the house party. Among the staff were Philip's detective Chief Inspector Trestrail, his valet Joe Pierce, Mrs Hazell and myself. We were the kitchen party. (Mrs Hazell was the housekeeper. She was not only a Treasure, she was a royal Treasure, a positive wonder for whom nothing was too much trouble.)

The kitchen party was responsible for preparing the evening meal, and we had the assistance, if that is the word, of the admiral's wife. But if ever there was a case of too many (amateur) cooks spoiling the broth, and practically everything else as well...

Mrs Hazell was nominally in charge, but it's not all that easy to command royal princes, an admiral and his wife, for a start. My job was to prepare the apple pie with Joe Pierce. Now I may not be too good at preparing *canard à l'orange* or *paupiettes de veau*, but my apple pie is good enough for an American mother. Between us, Joe and I produced an apple pie that was fit for a queen's consort. Under the approving eye of Mrs Hazell we put it into the eye-level oven that seemed to have enough controls to send it into orbit. Mrs Hazell was perfectly at home with this technological triumph of its time and set the controls.

A little later, enter Mrs Bonham-Carter. Apparently she looked through the glass door of the oven and saw a beautifully browned apple pie. She switched off the oven and took out the pie just in time to stop it burning.

Much later, after the meal, the dirty dishes started to come into the kitchen. (The exalted guests who had enjoyed themselves 'helping' to prepare the meal presumably considered that they had done enough. The rest of us could have the pleasure of washing up. They contented themselves with bringing in the crocks. Informality has its limits.)

The Duke of Edinburgh brought in my lovely apple pie. To my considerable surprise and chagrin I saw that only one piece had been cut from it, and that was lying on the rest of the pie. The Duke commented that the best part had been the partially cooked apple; the crust had been a little too much for normal teeth. I tried a piece, and I had to admit that it could have been used for boot soles, if anyone could have got nails through it.

Eventually we realized that Mrs Bonham-Carter, with the best will in the world but absolutely no expertise, thinking she was saving the pie from burning, had taken the pie from the oven when just the top of the crust had browned, long before the pie had been properly cooked. I hope her husband ran the Navy better.

Another of Charles's favourite estates for shooting-parties was at the Stansted, Essex, home of Aubrey Buxton MC, later Baron Buxton of Alsa. His friendship with the royal family was unsurprising in view of his background. Among many other things he was a former Trinity man, a director of Anglia Television, a former extra equerry to the Duke of Edinburgh, British Trustee of the World Wildlife Fund, founder of Stansted Wildlife Park, producer of sixty of Anglia TV's wildlife films and author of numerous articles on exploration and wildlife. Since then his awards and appointments have greatly increased.

It was during one of Charles's shoots at Stansted that I unexpectedly gained a rare viewpoint of game-shooting. Charles and I set off from Cambridge in the Land Rover on a very foggy day. We were late leaving because the fog had delayed the delivery of his daily bag of his private correspondence – as opposed to the occasional red box containing State documents for his attention as senior Counsellor of State, which he had become on his eighteenth birthday. Rather than delay any longer while he studied his letters and replied to the urgent ones, he decided to take the bag with him and work on them during the journey.

At Stansted Charles went to find the shooting-party, which had already left the house. Meanwhile I took the bag to Bishop's Stortford railway station to put it on the London train. By the time I got back to the Buxton home the fog had thickened and there was no sign of the guns. I asked Mrs (later Lady) Buxton where the party had gone.

'Oh, they're over there,' she said, with a wave that was graceful but almost totally uninformative.

I decided to follow the advice of the general who said 'Ride towards the sound of the guns!' I drove off slowly, and the sound of shooting came closer and closer, but I could still couldn't see anyone. After a while I got out of the Land Rover for a better look.

I heard a sharp rattle on the side of the Land Rover and realized with a shock that they were shotgun pellets. I was out of sight, but not out of range. All of a sudden I was, in a manner of speaking, with the birdies. I knew what it was to be on the wrong end of a shotgun.

I leapt into the Land Rover, reversed out hurriedly and found my way back to the house.

I was sitting reading a magazine when Mrs Buxton walked in and saw me.

'Oh, back already?' she said, surprised. I explained what had happened. 'Oh, I shouldn't worry,' she said airily. 'We've only ever lost one beater like that.'

At least I came off better than a certain pheasant during a shoot at the estate of Sir Michael Adeane (now Lord Adeane), private secretary to the Queen, near the River Deben in East Anglia. The beaters drove the birds towards the guns, where they flew into a barrage that must have equalled the flak over the Ruhr during the war. All except one pheasant, who acted as if he knew the rules of sportsmanship about shooting only birds on the wing. This bird walked determinedly towards Prince Philip, resisting all the efforts of the beaters to make it take off. Philip was muttering very democratic words that risked taking the sheen off his shotgun, cursing the bird for refusing to fly. It walked steadily on.

Philip finally lost patience, saying something like 'You've had your blanking chance', and shot the pheasant as it waddled on towards him.

I felt for that bird.

I frequently drove Charles over to Stansted with some of his friends. One of these was Cindy, one of the Buxtons' daughters, now a television producer. Although the inevitable newspaper gossip included her as one of the long list of women enjoying a romance with Charles, they were good friends, and nothing more.

Occasionally Charles and Anne went for a weekend shoot and riding at Lord Abergavenny's estate at Eridge, near Royal Tunbridge Wells in Kent. It was about seventeen miles from Princess Anne's school, Benenden, near Cranbrook. I went there to pick her up and take her to Eridge.

Another estate where I believe Charles went shooting was that of James Robertson-Justice in Sutherland. I know that he wrote politely, and with great respect for protocol, inviting Charles and Anne to his estate for shooting.

Best known to the general public as an actor, mainly in the *Doctor in the House* films, Robertson-Justice was rather more than that. In fact he was entitled to call himself 'Doctor', although not a doctor of medicine.

James Norval Harald Robertson-Justice described himself as having an undistinguished but varied career with some sixty-odd jobs in various parts of the world, and was proud of his invention of a rocket-propelled net method for catching wildfowl – not for killing them but for marking them. His hobby was falconry, his interests ornithology, ecology and conservation, subjects on which he had written a number of papers. His education at Marlborough College and Bonn University, where he took a PhD in Natural Sciences, helped to make him an extremely interesting conversationalist.

Robertson-Justice was always properly conscious of Prince Charles's position, and Charles soon made people aware of it if they were overstepping the boundaries into over-familiarity. Nevertheless, there was a powerful genuine bonhomie about Robertson-Justice which allowed him to say things without offence that would have been *lèse-majesté* in most other people.

This was demonstrated on one of the frequent trips when I accompanied Charles to London from Scotland on the *Royal Highlander*, a night sleeper train. We were having a meal in the restaurant car. As usual we had an end table and I sat with my back to the kitchen so that I could keep the whole of the carriage under observation, as I always did in public places. Charles, of course, had his back to the carriage but occasionally looked over his shoulder to see what was going on behind him.

The far door of the carriage opened and a massive,

unmistakable figure filled it. James Robertson-Justice carefully moved towards us, extravagantly gesturing to me not to give him away. He was over-acting so vigorously with nods, winks and 'shushing' gestures that I found it hard not to laugh and give the game away. Instead, I animatedly talked to Charles to keep his attention and stop him turning round.

Robertson-Justice clapped a massive hand on the Prince's shoulder, making him jump, and boomed 'And how are you, my good man?' as he sat down next to him. There weren't many people who could have got away with it.

'I have a bottle of excellent port in my compartment. Why don't we go back there and share it?'

'Even better, we have a day compartment,' Charles said. 'Let's drink it there. Get the glasses, Varney.'

When I was first assigned to the protection of one particular member of the royal family, I suppose I was prepared for periods when I should have to put in long hours of duty. It was one of the prices to pay for the honour, and the interest, of being a member of the Royal Protection Unit. The reality was harsher than I had imagined, and there were times when I had to work without a break for as long as the oppressed slaves of our modern society, junior hospital doctors.

I remember an occasion when we set out from Trinity College for a shoot at Thetford, in Norfolk, where Charles was a guest at the Shadwell Park estate of Sir John Musker. He was a banker, a Cambridge graduate and a member of three exclusive clubs: White's, the Royal Yacht Squadron and the Jockey Club Rooms at Newmarket.

Charles drove me in his MGC the thirty-five miles or so to Thetford, where we arrived in time for a snatched breakfast of tea and toast. It was a particularly cold, wet day, and the lack of a solid breakfast made it seem all the colder out in the fields. At about 12.30 p.m. the guns broke off for a little light lunch before resuming action about an hour later. I was beginning to be thankful that we would be getting into a warm car when the day's shooting was over, even though it meant we would be setting off on a longish drive for London.

We arrived at Buckingham Palace at about a quarter to

seven, still dressed in our damp shooting-clothes. After the drive in a car with the heater going full blast we were beginning to steam gently. I just had time to rush upstairs to Chief Superintendent Perkins's office and brief him on all the latest incidents at Cambridge since my last report. From the palace I then dashed to the police section house in Ambrosden Avenue, changed into a dinner jacket and hurried off to Clarence House, where the Queen Mother had invited Prince Charles and some other guests to dinner. The meal was almost over by the time I got there, and I joined the party which went on to the London Palladium for the Royal Variety Performance. It was, as ever, a marvellous show, but I'm afraid that during the quieter moments of the show – and there weren't many – I found myself dozing, only to be woken abruptly by a great blast of music or wave of applause. Charles, on the other hand, was all bright-eyed and in fine form.

Shortly before 11.00 p.m. Charles, his equerry Squadron Leader Checketts (now Sir David Checketts) and I left the Palladium for Euston Station to catch the overnight train to Glasgow. It must have looked like something out of *Bulldog Drummond* or *Murder on the Orient Express* when three of us in evening dress strode up the platform to our sleeping compartments.

When we travelled to Scotland by train it was on either the *Royal Highlander* or the *Aberdonian*. We made so many trips that I got to know practically every sleeping-car attendant on the routes. But on this occasion there was no familiar attendant to play cards with, and I had nothing to read. Despite the title, I always slept badly in a railway sleeping compartment. Perhaps things are better these days, but then the compartments were like small, noisy, bouncing saunas, and nothing I did to the heating controls would bring down the temperature. So, I gloomily looked forward to another sleepless night of utter boredom with nothing to do. It seemed to last as long as a journey on the Trans-Siberian Railway.

At Glasgow we were met by officials from John Brown Ltd and driven to their shipyard, where we were taken on board the *Queen Elizabeth II*, which was in dry dock.

However well you may think you are prepared for your

first sight of the *Queen Elizabeth II* you are overwhelmed the first time you see her. She is huge, and seemed to me as big as half of Piccadilly. The initial impact was staggering.

Fortunately our first stop was at the dining-room, where we had breakfast, for this was the first time I had eaten anything since the light lunch at Thetford the previous day. Although I was keen enough to see as much as possible of the ship, I was rather reluctant to leave the table. At another time and in another place I should have tried to sneak a couple of slices of toast away with me.

After leaving the main dining room the party toured the various cabins, suites and shops. Below decks it was difficult to remember that we were actually on a ship, everything was on such a magnificent scale. To describe the potential luxury of the Penthouse Suite would have taxed the abilities of the most extravagant estate agent. In fact the price of the suite for a world cruise a few years ago was $309,000 – £216,000 at the then rate of exchange.

Throughout the tour of the accommodation and service areas, ending on the promenade deck, Charles displayed his usual interest and asked our guides a stream of questions. However, it was the vessel's massive bridge with all its most modern equipment which really fascinated him. Although he perhaps was not as technologically minded as his father he could not fail to be impressed by the control centre of this floating city.

Charles was on the bridge when the floodlit liner moved out of the shipyard at nine o'clock in the morning, seven tugs chuffing energetically around her, bound for Inchgreen Dry Dock, fourteen miles downriver at Greenock. The liner was going for fitting out, followed by sea trials after about a month. Charles waved to thousands of sightseers on the shore who had been waiting since early morning.

It was, I suppose, the end of an era. Even then most people realized that there was little chance of another one of the great Transatlantic-type liners being built there.

As the great ship sailed majestically down the Clyde towards Greenock you couldn't have got Charles away from the bridge with a crowbar. It was one of the most exciting trips I had ever made with him, because of the sense of occasion. As we slowly made our way downriver we were accompanied at a respectful distance by a horde of craft of all shapes and sizes, sounding their sirens in salute.

When the liner left her berth her bows scraped the side of a wharf, leaving a twenty-foot scratch on the paintwork. At the other end of the trip, the Scott Lithgow dry dock, she swung again and scratched the paintwork on the starboard side. I asked Charles 'Were you driving?'. I don't think he heard me. (In view of the way the day ended, it was an apposite remark.)

I very nearly didn't make the trip downriver. Before we got underway I was wandering around the promenade deck which had heavy glass panels between vertical struts instead of a solid metal or wooden barrier, a construction that provided an interrupted view. As we were in dry dock I wondered just how high we were. I walked to the side with my hand in front of me to feel for the glass panel.

There *wasn't* a panel.

Suddenly I was all too aware that I was very high up indeed. I was off-balance, and I could feel myself beginning to fall. I flung out my arms, and hit one of the vertical supports. I grabbed it, and managed to push myself back upright. One of the guides turned round at that moment and saw me holding onto the support.

'Look out!' he warned sharply. 'You'll fall over if you're not careful! There's no glass there.'

'Yes, I know,' I said, hoping my voice wasn't too shaky.

Later that long day we returned to London on a British European Airways flight from Abbotsinch. Sir Basil Smallpiece, the then chairman of BEA, accompanied us on the flight and sat next to Charles. They had a long conversation in which I took no part. I was having a conversation of my own with one of the stewardesses. I wasn't going to miss a chance to chat up an attractive young woman: opportunities were rare enough with the sort of life I was leading as Charles's detective.

In London Charles met Princess Anne for a visit to the Royal Festival Hall with two of her friends. I fought and won a difficult battle to keep my eyes open: I had hardly slept at all on the train the previous night. For all that I know, the performance could have been Japanese No theatre. From there we went to Buckingham Palace to await the Queen's arrival on the last stage of her journey from Brazil. Charles was keen to see his mother because he wouldn't have another chance for several weeks.

The Prince and I set off for Cambridge at about three a.m. in his MGC, with him at the wheel. In Charles's first days as a driver on public roads the way he drove kept his passengers very much wide-eyed and awake. After a journey with him most people got out of the car with an aching right leg, caused by pressing down hard on the floorboards on an imaginary brake. Some people take Dramamine to make a journey more comfortable; for a trip with Charles beta-blockers and Valium were more suitable.

Although I had become fairly hardened and fatalistic after a number of trips with him, as we came up to West Hampstead, the car behaved even more erratically than usual. I sat up when we narrowly missed a traffic bollard, and when the car headed for the pavement I glanced at Prince Charles and saw that he was driving with his eyes shut. I gave him a hefty nudge, which woke him.

'I'll drive,' I said. He yawned and stopped the car so I could take over. The shock he'd given me kept me wide awake for the rest of the journey. We got back to Cambridge at about a quarter past four. You had to be young and healthy to keep up with Charles at that time, even if you ended up feeling old and knackered.

It was a couple of days I have never forgotten. There were times enough when keeping up with Prince Charles was exhausting: unlike him I was unable to relax as I was responsible for his safety. However, these forty-eight-odd hours were the most tiring I have ever experienced, before or since.

During one of the vacations at Cambridge Charles was given a flight at RAF Tangmere, one of the famous Battle of Britain aerodromes. He found the experience so enjoyable that he decided to learn to fly. Also while on vacation he took some lessons, as I recall, at RAF White Waltham, which is not far from Windsor. When he returned to Trinity he was determined to keep up his flying, even though he was working very hard for his degree and was constantly being involved in all sorts of extra-mural activities and distractions.

Whenever he could find time from his studies and the weather was fit for flying Charles went to RAF Oakington for lessons. His instructor, Squadron Leader Philip Pinney, a New Zealander, came over from RAF Benson to take him up in a Chipmunk training aircraft. While he was airborne I could not accompany him, of course, and I spent most of my time playing cards with the ground crew. I suppose RAF ground crews do a lot of waiting around for aircraft to return, which gives them the opportunity to sharpen their card-playing skills. Certainly I found playing cards with them an expensive distraction. And, although I thought about it very hard, unfortunately there was no way I could claim expenses for my losses.

They were a great bunch of lads, and they always did everything they possibly could to make sure Charles got the most from his limited flying-time. Every time we drove over to Oakington he was always buoyed up at the thought of flying; on the way back he frequently said how exciting and exhilarating he found it. He spoke, too, of the sense of freedom it gave him.

Anyone who had spent any time with Charles would be completely unsurprised that he found flying fascinating. So often he had enjoyed going off on his own – except for me, tagging along – sailing, fishing or simply tramping through the countryside. He was self-sufficient and happy in his own company, away from all the pressures on him: the press, people wanting to meet him, people wanting something from him, and perhaps the most weighty of all the pressures, the imperative to be successful because of who he was and what he would become. So, being alone in the sky with – for the moment anyway – no one to make demands on him, and no responsibilities to fulfil must have been a marvellous feeling for him.

One day when we turned up at Oakington Squadron Leader Pinney winked at me and said, out of Charles's earshot, 'Today's the day'. The Prince didn't know it yet, but he was about to go solo. He had done about fourteen hours dual instruction before Pinney decided he was fit to go off on his own. I've no doubt Charles could have managed it sooner, but you don't take risks with the heir to the throne. Unfortunately the weather was poor, with lots of low cloud about. So the Squadron Leader flew off in the Chipmunk with Charles to see if he could find a break in the weather. Charles still didn't know why his instructor was so keen to get in some flying on this gloomy day. At nearby RAF Bassingbourne the weather was fit for his first 'circuit and bump' – the RAF expression for a practice take-off and landing.

I learned afterwards that Squadron Leader Pinney landed, taxied the Chipmunk to the end of the runway, then got out, saying to Charles with a friendly lack of protocol, 'You're on your own, mate.'

When Charles returned to Oakington I knew him well enough to see that he was delighted, even though he was playing it cool. He was thrilled with his first solo, of course. Later he said 'I only had time for a few butterflies in the stomach. The moment I was in the air, it was absolutely marvellous.'

12   Abroad with Ark and Ant

Unlikely as it may seem, there was little I actually envied Charles. Of course, as a moderately paid police constable I did envy his total lack of concern about money as a member of one of the richest families in the world. The one thing I did envy him was his overseas travel. I accompanied him on only one trip, to France and Jersey. It was a private trip to give him a chance to extend his archaeological and anthropological studies.

Charles clearly enjoyed the excursion apart from a couple of minor incidents, but for me – and, I suspect, for some of the other members of our party – it was a week of extremely mixed feelings. In the party were Dr John Coles, his director of studies, Squadron Leader Checketts and Dr Glyn Daniel, from St John's College at Cambridge. Dr Daniel was an was a learned and respected academic who had written a number of important books on archaeology. However, he was well known to the general public outside academic circles because he was a major television personality of the time who appeared regularly on the highly popular BBC programme *Animal, Vegetable, Mineral.* In addition to his home in Cambridge he had another in the Pas de Calais area of France.

As it was a private trip Charles had no State visits to make or meetings to attend. Nevertheless, when we travelled or stayed anywhere, it was hardly like a small family outing. Apart from Charles himself, Dr Daniel, Dr Cole, Squadron Leader Checketts and myself, there were three gendarmes (local policemen), three officers from the *Sureté Nationale* in

Paris and two chauffeurs. That was our party. We travelled
in two British Embassy cars, preceded by one police car and
sometimes with another bringing up the rear.

In France we had no problems with the general public:
Charles's presence in the country went virtually unnoticed by
the locals. Those that did see him by chance probably didn't
recognize him. In fact, even if people had known he was
there and they wanted to get to see him, they wouldn't have
managed to get near him, past the barrier of the press corps.
At most places the French and British journalists outnumbered the public by about three to one. The press constantly
trailed behind like a horde of motorized camp followers.
Sometimes, when they were afraid of losing us down a side
road or in traffic, they kept so close that it seemed that the
leader was trying to get into the boot of our last car.

The French motorized police are justly renowned for their
high degree of skill, as anyone who has seen Parisian
motorcycle policemen weaving through heavy traffic,
opening up the way for official cars, will know. They often
appear to take chances that would get one of our own
motorcycle policeman arrested.

There was one occasion in France when Charles was given
a demonstration of their capabilities which he thoroughly
appreciated. We were driving along a straightish main road
with no half-concealed side roads, so the press cars for once
were staying at a reasonable distance behind us. On a parallel
road, maybe a quarter of a mile away, there was a large
military convoy of heavy vehicles, more or less keeping level
with us.

Without warning our leading car suddenly accelerated, and
the rest of our group sped off after it in a race to where the
two roads converged and crossed.

It was beautifully judged, like a well-rehearsed sequence
from a film.

The last of our cars shot across the bows of the leading
vehicle of the military convoy, effectively cutting us off from
the gaggle of press cars behind us.

We all gave a small cheer; Charles himself was clearly
delighted by the incident. Not that it meant we had
completely shaken off the journalists: they knew where we
were going, and simply turned up a little late. Nevertheless,

it was a small but welcome victory. By this time Charles had become fairly accustomed to press attention and had developed, at least outwardly, a philosophical approach it, although there were times when his patience was sorely tried on this trip.

On a number of occasions I asked the French police accompanying us whether they couldn't do something about the number of journalists and photographers who were constantly tracking us.

The reaction was always much the same: an apologetic smile, a Gallic shrug and an explanation that they couldn't tell the Pressmen to buzz off because they would immediately start complaining that the police were behaving like Fascists. Before I left for France I had been told that the French police don't enjoy nearly as friendly relations with the public as British police do – and God knows that's far from friendly sometimes. If journalists started yelling that the police were acting like a bunch of Fascists towards them, most people would be only too ready to believe them. The French press, too, seemed to have a much stronger sense of their own importance – no, 'of their own *authority*' is nearer the truth. They expected to be given licence to get stories any way they could.

The first night of our stay in France was spent at Les Eyzies in the Dordogne. Les Eyzies is near the Grotte de Lascaux with its world-famous, quite unparalleled Cro-Magnon cave paintings; and also close to the cave at Les Combarelles with its engraved designs which suggest that it served as the centre of a hunting cult over a long period. Scholars generally agree that Les Combarelles is one of the finest products of the Ice Age.

Our first night in Les Eyzies was a fairly lively affair. At dinner Charles shared a table with Checketts, while the rest of us – local and Paris police and chauffeurs – shared a table. As the meal progressed each of us in turn bought a different bottle of wine. We told ourselves it was as a tribute to the wine-growers of this area rich in good wines. By the end of the evening I doubt that we would have noticed whether or not we were drinking Algerian red or even cooking sherry. Our meal lasted from seven o'clock until one o'clock the following morning, and by the end it had become fairly boisterous. I think that Charles, abstemious as ever, felt a little frosty towards us. Squadron Leader Checketts kept aiming dark looks at us but they bounced off us like ping-pong balls against a brick wall.

Despite having taken on board a fair amount of wine I was still in full control of myself when we all turned in. It was just as well, for I had the opportunity to get my own back on the press in a most satisfying way for some of the irritations we had to put up with. You might say I struck a blow for our party.

We had taken an entire floor at Hôtel Les Glycines, a pleasant, comfortable place, rather off the beaten track. At least, the intention was to have a floor to ourselves. In fact we did not have the entire floor at Les Glycines. A woman journalist from *Paris Match*, who gave me her name as Mlle de la Brosse, had obviously had been given a tip-off that Prince Charles and his party were going to stay at the hotel. Well in advance of his arrival she took a room on the floor that was meant to be reserved for us, and then refused to budge when the management wanted her to go. A journalist with *Paris Match* had a great deal of clout, and I am sure she threatened the hotel she would use it. She was still there when we turned up.

Charles had a room in the middle of the central corridor; mine was at the staircase end of it. I slept with my door open, while at the far end from me sat a *gendarme*, keeping watch throughout the night. At about 2 a.m., I suppose it was, something made me wake up: I assumed it was a movement in the corridor. I slipped out of bed and quietly looked round my door. The *gendarme* wasn't at his post. (We subsequently established that he had moved away for a few moments to go to the loo.)

Outside Prince Charles's room, bending down to look through the keyhole, was Mlle de la Brosse. Clearly she had been biding her time, waiting for the *gendarme* to leave for a while, as he was bound to have to at some time during the entire night after all the food and drink we had put away.

Goodness only knows what she expected to see in a dark room through the keyhole, unless, of course, she was hoping to make out two figures in the bed – or even better, hoping that a discreet light would reveal two people engrossed in each other.

As she peered through the keyhole, her *peignoir* was stretched tightly over her shapely bottom. It was a temptation I had no intention whatsoever of resisting. She was concentrating so hard on trying to see through the darkness that she was unaware of my approach. I had to judge my action fairly precisely: hard enough to sting, but not hard enough to make a loud noise or startle her into crying out so that Charles would be woken.

And then I gave her a most satisfying, solid smack on the backside, harder than I had meant to, producing a resounding 'Thwack!'.

I give Mlle de la Brosse her due. She leapt upright, but had enough presence of mind not to cry out. I gave her a sweet smile and wagged my finger at her. Without a word she turned away and went to her room. There was no sound from inside Charles's room.

I didn't sleep much that night, in case she tried a second time, although with the *gendarme* at the end of the corridor alerted to her antics, it was highly unlikely. Next morning Charles remarked that I looked rather washed out. He asked me what I'd been doing.

'Having contact with the press,' I said. He gave me that famous quizzical look, but I don't think he ever knew what had happened.

The caves at Lascaux were discovered in 1940 by four boys who were looking for their dog. The main cavern and various galleries were decorated with paintings, drawings and engravings of various animals. The paintings were done on a light background in different shades of black, brown, red and yellow. They were in almost perfect condition when the cave was first found, but when it was opened up to the public the carbon dioxide exhaled by the visitors caused the rich colours to fade, and a green fungus began to form over some of the paintings. So, the cave was closed in 1963, just three years before Charles's visit. The authorities offered to open up the cave for him, but he refused. His concern for the paintings was greater than his personal curiosity. (His interest in archaeology and anthropology was genuine: he didn't read the subjects simply because he had to read something at Cambridge and 'ark and ant' were as good as anything. He also had then, as he clearly has now, a profound concern for the environment.)

Our next stop was at Saumur on the River Loire in western France. The town, which is dominated by the imposing fourteenth century château of the dukes of Anjou, is famous for its wines and the celebrated cavalry school.

Charles, a polo player and a member of a horse-loving family – if not horse-obsessed in one or two cases – was fascinated by the cavalry school and stayed two nights there as the guest of Major Tubbs. This meant that I had some time to myself, because it was fair to assume that Charles would be fairly well protected with all those cavalry officers round him. Normally there aren't all that many anti-royalists in cavalry units.

I was staying at the Hôtel Budan with Dr Glyn Daniel. One evening this learned academic took the trouble to give me some invaluable instruction. He introduced me to the delights of fine food and superb wine. Not only did he guide me through an magnificent dinner, he regaled me with brilliant conversation. It was an experience I have never forgotten.

During the day I had bought a picture postcard from the museum at Les Eyzies. It was of large statue outside the museum of a Cro-Magnon man. He isn't very handsome. Dr Daniel's superb dinner had made me mellower than a Stradivarius violin, and I had the bright idea of addressing the card to Chief Superintendent Perkins with the message, 'Having a wonderful time. I see they've erected a statue to you here.' (I'm pretty sure that Dr Daniel egged me on a little.) The next morning I looked at the card not believing that I actually intended to send it. I couldn't imagine what Chief Superintendent Perkins would have said. On second thoughts, I could; I never accused him of having a sense of humour.

It was on this trip that, for the only time I was with Prince Charles, that I was completely floored by a question from a journalist. Normally I didn't have much to do with newspaper people. It was my job to remain in the background, and they took little enough notice of me, which suited me perfectly. However, the expedition to France was rather out of the ordinary because our party was easily approached.

A woman journalist asked me outright: 'Do you know when Prince Charles lost his virginity?'

I was totally taken aback by the sheer brazenness of the question. I must have cut a sorry figure as I stood mumbling inaudibly. It wasn't that I didn't know the answer, which could have been a simple 'Yes' or 'No' – although a great deal could be inferred even from one of those one-word answers. It was the sheer brassbound effrontery of the question, put in a reasonable tone and with a pleasant smile. Somehow it seemed to me that trying to peer through the keyhole of his bedroom door was less crass and insensitive. Anyway, the journalist concerned was going to get no satisfaction or clues from me. And nor was anyone else. As far as I was and am concerned, when, where and with whom Charles lost his virginity (or gave it away) was no one's business but his own...and the woman's.

I was sorry to leave France. Visiting the warm, sunny Dordogne – which had not become the In place with the British at that time – was very different from tramping about Scottish moors and Fenlands in mists and penetrating cold. Charles, too, was having the time of his life, it seemed. Although he had seen some marvellous places throughout the world, here in France, and later in Jersey, he was able to indulge his genuine passion for archaeology at one of the world's most fascinating sites. It seemed to me, too, that he was conscious that the days of freedom of university life were diminishing: the shades of the prison-house were beginning to close upon the growing boy.

After the relatively – *relatively* – easy and comfortable time we had in France, Jersey was a very different matter altogether. Charles had the advantage of us all in that he had learned to rough it at an early age when he was at Gordonstoun and Timbertop: he was physically and mentally far better prepared than the rest of us. The conditions in Jersey were Boy Scout or armed services stuff: the party lived in tents near a cliff edge – but not near enough to be dangerous – from where Charles could go every day to take part in an archaeological dig in a cave.

The tents were pitched on private land belonging to a Mr and Mrs McBurnie. All our water had to be carried down from the house, while our loos were ordinary camp latrines:

trenches dug in the ground. The McBurnies' daughter brought us food which we prepared on primus stoves and barbecues. Gone were the days of hotel food and wine, of hot baths and showers, of someone doing the laundry and making the beds...

Before we arrived the Lieutenant-Governor and Commander-in-Chief – the same person – asked the inhabitants to respect Prince Charles's privacy, and by and large they did so. The only slight problem we had with sightseers was on our arrival at the airport.

In the hope that it would keep press interest to a minimum for the four days Charles and his party would be in Jersey, an open day for the press was laid on. During the course of that day our party and the visiting pressmen had to walk along a narrow path uncomfortably close to the edge of a 200-foot drop with some unpleasant-looking rocks below. I was just behind the photographer Ray Bellisario when suddenly he turned and looked at me with a pale, strained face.

'I know you're planning to kill me,' he said.

To put the situation in its proper context I have to go back a few years to explain the experiences the royal family and their protection officers – including myself – had suffered because of Bellisario.

Of all the journalists and photographers I had encountered during my service with the Royal Protection Group, undoubtedly the most persistent – for 'persistent' read 'pestilential' – was Bellisario, who specialized in 'candid' photographs of members of the royal family.

One of his exploits was really rather amusing, even though the joke was on me. Prince Charles's *Macbeth* played to full houses; when he was due to appear in *The Footlights Revue* at Cambridge the interest was even more intense, if that is possible. A royal prince playing a king in a Shakespeare play is one thing, but any theatre would be filled by the same prince cavorting in a revue where dignity would be almost as rare as community singing in a Trappist monastery. The theatre was packed.

Inevitably there were a lot of young women there anxious to see Prince Charles and, with a little luck, to be seen by him. Some of them made my eyes pop. They had absolutely stupendously oversized busts: but that wasn't the only cause

of my astonishment. Their shapes were contrary to all physio-
logical and natural laws. They were like a battleship's big
guns: ponderous, pointing upwards and outwards at totally
unbelievable angles. I had to assume that the latest craze
among the college girls was for padded bras. The only other
explanation I could find was that there was a hitherto un-
known phalanx of Jayne Mansfields in Cambridge or that a
cut-price plastic surgeon was operating in the district. Still, I
couldn't give too much thought to this extraordinary outbreak. I was more concerned with the fact that Ray Bellisario
was in Cambridge.

The lure – and challenge – of snatching off-guard pictures of
Charles in costume or possibly in an unflattering situation
would be irresistible to the little Italian photographer. Pictures
like that would be worth a great deal of money to one of the
tabloids.

When he turned up, as I knew he would, I met him at the
door.

'Hello, Mr Varney,' Bellisario said affably. 'Look, I'm
legitimate.' Being the man he was, he had managed to wangle
a ticket from someone. He handed it to me with a smile so
innocent that it was obvious he was up to something. 'No
camera tonight,' he went on. 'Search me if you like.'

There was no need for the invitation. I was going to search
him whether he liked it or not. I did so very thoroughly,
twice, and I was not surprised that I found nothing. Bellisario
was on his own, so he had no one to sneak a camera in for him.
I looked to see where he was sitting, but there was no one near
him who looked even remotely likely to be smuggling in a
camera to pass on to him. Perhaps, after all, he was having an
evening off.

As soon as Charles came onto the stage all the big-busted
young women dived into their bras and dragged out cameras.
There were flashes going off all over the theatre and there was
nothing I could do about it. I glared at Bellisario. He smiled
back at me, but with much less innocence. It was obvious that
the photographers were all members of the Bellisario army.
He knew perfectly well that I wouldn't search in the women's
bras.

Totally unamusing and, in my view, sordidly prurient, was
one of his earlier coups.

Bellisario's particular targets were the princesses, and because of him they had to take extraordinary precautions whenever they were on holiday. Before they went swimming or sunbathing the grounds even of private houses had to be scoured to make sure that he wasn't lurking there.

And for good reason, after Princess Alexandra's experience. When she was on her honeymoon in April 1963 Bellisario climbed up a tree and stayed there for hours, his camera trained on her bedroom window. The Princess undoubtedly thought she could count on privacy and was not as prudent as she might have been near the windows. Bellisario was rewarded – if that is the word – with some revealing photographs. This was his most unforgivable exploit, as far as most of the royal family and household were concerned. Princess Alexandra, a most charming lady, second in popularity only to the Queen Mother, was and is a warm favourite with everyone.

Almost equally high on the animosity scale was the general reaction to Bellisario's photographs of Princess Margaret water-skiing on Sonning Water. Lord Snowdon never forgave him for it. Incidentally, a profound dislike of Bellisario was one of the few things that Prince Philip and Lord Snowdon had in common. 'Tony's' almost obsessional detestation of the photographer, as I saw it, gave rise to an interesting incident which provided an insight into Princess Margaret's husband.

It occurred when I was accompanying Charles back to Gordonstoun for the summer term of his last year at the school on a flight in an Andover from Heathrow to Lossiemouth. The Snowdons had an engagement in Glasgow and shared the aircraft with Charles. As we took off from London Airport we were all securely seated with our seat belts on...all except Lord Snowdon, that is. He remained standing, teetering a little on braced legs, trying to get a sight of Sonning Water. Suddenly he lost his balance and came tumbling backwards, crashing into the seat next to me.

I'm human. I couldn't quite keep a smile off my face.

Later his valet, Richard, came to me and said, 'His Lordship wants to know why you didn't stand up when he sat down next to you on the plane.'

'He's joking, of course,' I said, when I got my breath back.

'Oh, no. He's very serious,' Richard said.

When thinking of Bellisario and Sonning Water, Lord Snowdon's sense of humour had a flat battery.

Soon after the deplorable incident of the Princess Alexandra photographs I was with Prince Charles at Balmoral. The ubiquitous Bellisario was in the vicinity, at the Craigendarroch Hotel in Ballater, just down the road. Several of our off-duty royal policemen were in the hotel bar when someone suggested that it would be a good idea to throw Bellisario into the nearby River Dee.

We began to reminisce about all the underhand tricks he had pulled on members of the royal family and the problems that he had caused us in the past: cancelled leaves, cold nights in lonely grounds, inquiries and rockets when things went wrong. We had worked up a good head of steam when in walked Bellisario.

He saw us at once, and hesitated for a second, like an early Christian who had just noticed that he had walked into an arena full of hungry lions. He must have had an almost overwhelming urge to turn round and walk out again, but to his credit, he strolled up to us, and managed a smile. It was a pretty fair exhibition of moral courage.

'What are you drinking?' he asked.

All I had to do was nod, and he would have been in the Dee, but I hadn't the heart for it. I had to give the devil his due for his nerve. I said quietly something like, 'You've just had narrow escape. This time.'

To return to Jersey: when Bellisario said, 'I know you're planning to kill me,' I had forgotten about this meeting a few years earlier. I was completely taken aback that anyone should think that my protection of Prince Charles went as far as killing undesirables. I'm sure he totally misinterpreted my obvious surprise. I simply couldn't believe he could be so daft, but he probably thought I was disconcerted at having my murderous plan found out.

'I've been warned, and I've left a note with a friend,' he continued. 'If I don't come back because I've had an 'accident', he'll hand the note to the local police.' As an added warning he went on: 'And remember, they still hang murderers out here.'

I was on the point of playing him along by saying in a cynical tone, 'They might suspect, but they could never prove anything', when I saw that Bellisario was genuinely scared that I might heave him out into space. Instead, I tried to explain that someone must have been pulling his leg. I tried to draw him aside but he refused to budge. I stretched out my hand and patted him with what I thought was a friendly gesture, but he steadied himself, preparing to resist a shove. So I tried a friendly smile, but it must have come out all wrong, because Bellisario recoiled.

Then I remembered my words of a couple of years previously. *'You've had a narrow escape. This time.'* It was clear that I shouldn't be able to persuade him I meant no harm.

Still, once again he displayed courage – physical courage this time. He turned his back on me and walked along the foot-wide path worn into the cliff-top with me behind him.

I subsequently discovered who had planted the thought in Bellisario's mind. One of Charles's party had a quiet word with him before we set out:

'We think it's only fair to warn you that Varney's been making threats against you. We think he's becoming a little unbalanced. We could be wrong...but just the same, you might be wise to stay with the main party at all times...so that there's no danger of him catching you alone on the cliff-edge.'

And the instigator? Prince Charles himself. He had managed to turn his penchant for practical jokes into a right royal revenge for some of the tricks Bellisario had pulled against the royal family.

It was strange that the normally introverted Charles should be such a practical joker. Maybe he felt that because of his position he could get away with it without fear of reprisal, but I'm almost certain it wasn't that. As long as I was with him Charles was concerned far less with the privileges of his position than with its duties and responsibilities. It's simply that he had a strong sense of humour that compensated for the seriousness of his life.

He started early as a joker: one of his earliest tricks was to slip an ice cube down an unsuspecting footman's neck at Buckingham Palace. Rather more daring, he tried to slip a whoopee cushion on the seat that was going to be occupied by the Bishop of Norwich on a visit to the palace. A number of palace servants mentioned that one to me, but no one knew how and from where Charles had got the cushion. At least, no one was owning up to it.

When he was at Timbertop he actually managed to con Aussies in Melbourne that the Timbertop boys had invented a new system for capturing kangaroos. They crept up on an unsuspecting beast, grabbed it by the tail and flipped it over onto its back, where it was helpless, he told the credulous Aussies.

A few of Charles's fellow 'ark and ant' students from Cambridge joined us in Jersey. There were about a dozen tents in our camp, set in a small hollow at the top of the cliffs on a point by Gros Nez Bay. Charles spent most of his time at the dig in the nearby La Cotte cave, but somehow I didn't seem to have all that much time to myself.

The irrepressible – there are other adjectives that would apply – Bellisario didn't respect the tacit agreement that Charles and his party be left alone by journalists and photographers in exchange for the open press day at the beginning of the trip. He decided that the best way to get through the police cordon round the camp would be to send two young women to climb up the cliff right beside the camp and snatch what pictures they could. He guessed that he was too well-known himself and that the local police would be keeping an eye on him. Two 'tourists' wouldn't attract anyone's attention until it was too late.

It was fairly smart thinking...except for one thing. There was no police cordon round the camp. Only me. Anyone could virtually have walked through the middle of the place.

We had no more trouble from Bellisario. I assumed that once he realized that just anyone could get photographs of the place he lost interest. His speciality was exclusive pictures that no one else could snatch. Or perhaps he really did think that given half a chance I would have him over the edge of the cliff.

Charles showed every sign that he was having a marvellous time during our stay in Jersey. He was indulging in one of his passions, 'ark and ant', and he was enormously enjoying the informality and freedom of the visit. Normally he preferred to be on his own as much as possible, but this time he seemed to be very happy to be with others.

Now I look back on the period, I find it almost incredible

that the whole stay in Jersey was so casual, and relatively so unprotected. Such a situation would be completely unimaginable today. My personal memories are of a pleasant, relaxed and undemanding time. However, shortly after our return to mainland Britain I saw myself ('Charles's long-suffering detective') quoted as saying, 'Believe me, this was no holiday. It's one of the hardest few days I've ever spent. I'd like to lie in the sun for a week to recover.' Well, *if* I said it, I must have been tired and emotional at the time.

Not long after the France and Jersey trip Charles reached another milestone in his life. It gave me an unexpected insight into his character. A number of times in this book I have mentioned that he was a highly complex and basically shy young man. Given his background, his experience of always being the centre of intense media attention, and the awful responsibility that would be his one day, his introversion was understandable. Being so close to him for so long made me aware of the tremendous pressures he had to bear. His desire to get away on his own into open spaces, away from constant demands, was only too understandable.

Yet there was one element of his make-up that had always baffled me.

Charles frequently seemed to under-estimate his own worth. Yet he was an achiever. Although he was not naturally gifted academically he got good examination results at Gordonstoun and at Cambridge in the teeth of the distractions of official duties and travels which bit deeply into his study time. He learned to fly, to sail, to play polo, to act, to play the cello...

The possible explanation of this seeming paradox struck me one evening while I was on leave, watching television. The newsreel showed Charles arriving at Windsor for his installation as a Knight of the Garter. I remember that in the procession with him were his beloved 'Uncle Dickie' – his great-uncle Earl Mounbatten of Burma, Viscount Alexander of Tunis and Viscount Montgomery of Alamein, among others. Then it dawned on me. Those other, mature men were there because of what they had done; the young Charles was there because of who he was. Had he been a dull wimp, he still would have taken his place among those great figures because of the accident of his birth. No matter what he did, he could never win the battle of achievement against rank.

As we have seen, Charles never had a great many close friends of his own age, largely for the reasons that he made clear himself: he could never be sure who was genuine and who was a phony. But there was more to it than that; much more. As I discovered myself when my tour of duty with him ended, it was not in his character to have many of the really deep friendships that many people enjoy. At least, he showed no sign of that sort of 'commitment', I suppose the word is, to any of his contemporaries during the seven years I was with him. It is all at one with the fact that from an early age Charles always seemed happier with those either considerably younger or considerably older than himself. He got on famously with children and with his grandmother, for example.

One of my own friends has a touchstone for deciding whether someone is a good friend or not. Could you ring him up at 3 a.m. and say you are stuck on the M1 fifty miles away and know he'd come out to pick you up?

Charles might well get half a dozen people to do that for him (if he needed to) for pretty obvious motives. But for how many people would *he* do it? I do not mean for a second that he was careless of other people's feelings or without concern for those in distress, but the capacity for that sort of commitment did not seem to be there. Maybe it was because that sort of friendship has to be strengthened by adversity, and real adversity was something that Charles could never know. The facts that he was necessarily brought up by paid servants and could have little enough contact with his parents because of their duties, and that he became aware of the uniqueness of his position from an early age, would help to diminish his potential for committed friendship. It's possible, perhaps even likely, that as he grew older and served in the Royal Navy, where they have long been unimpressed by members of royal families, he may have developed the capacity for stronger relationships.

Yet there was one man to whom Charles was devoted, whom he admired above everyone. For him Charles *would* have gone fifty miles to pick him up at 3 a.m.

Earl Mountbatten of Burma.

There is a saying that every father is a hero to his own son, and it is certain that Philip was a hero to Charles. In fact Philip was a *real* hero, not just a boy's idea of one: he served in the Navy during the shooting war in the Mediterranean and the Pacific. And from the moment when Charles was old enough to understand, he could see that his father had prestige and authority. When he spoke, people jumped. Crowds of people turned out to cheer him, even when he was on his own. Any boy would be in awe of a father like that.

Philip was a physical, athletic and active man, an extrovert, and he tried to mould Charles into his own image, to 'make a man of him'. Charles tried valiantly to please Philip, in this and every way. From what I saw of the father and son during my seven years and more, it was clear that Charles had enormous respect and admiration for his father. What other major emotion he may have felt for Philip was less evident.

Certainly his attitude to Lord Mountbatten and his manner when he was with him were quite different. All the qualities that made Philip a hero to Charles, Mountbatten possessed more generously – and he had others, too. As captain of a warship Mountbatten had an even more spectacular fighting record. He then rose steadily to be Chief of Combined Operations, Member of the Chiefs of Staff Committee and Supreme Commander, South-East Asia. (His connections and background were hardly a handicap to advancement, but he wouldn't have got that far without ability.) After the war he became Viceroy of India, where he was, by definition, the sovereign's direct representative.

There was something about this rank that Charles could not fail to see. His (macho) father must always take second place to the Queen; as Viceroy Mountbatten was the premier figure – his wife came after him in precedence.

Mountbatten was also a physical man – his naval service, his polo playing and underwater fishing prove that – but he was less obvious about it than Philip, and this lack of stridency must have appealed to Charles. The older man had other traits that struck a sympathetic chord in Charles. He was much more academically minded than Philip, who professed to feel that he was the better for not having gone to university. Charles was happy at Trinity, and Mountbatten had been a Cambridge man too. In fact he visited Charles at Trinity when he went to Cambridge to give the Nehru lecture.

Mountbatten was cultured, well read and fluent in French and German. Most of all, he was a historical figure in his own lifetime: he had influenced world affairs as Philip never could despite his rank. No wonder that Charles admired him intensely. Perhaps the relationship was not too one-sided for another reason: Mountbatten had no son.

There was one particular interest that Charles shared with 'Uncle Dickie'. They both enjoyed acting – or more accurately, performing, in its wider sense. Charles, as we know, had a great time on the stage. In the 1920s the then Lord Louis Mountbatten managed to get himself in front of amateur movie cameras with another Charles – Chaplin. The connection does not stop there. Mountbatten's son-in-law, Lord Brabourne, is a distinguished and successful film producer, and Lord Romsey (Norton Knatchbull) works in the film industry. Among Mountbatten's enormous list of official and unofficial appointments he was President of the Society of Film and Television Arts and a member of the Inner Magic Circle.

The reason for mentioning all this is not to provide a two-paragraph biography of Mountbatten but to underline some of the characteristics that drew Charles to him.

Incidentally, Mountbatten indirectly helped break the ice between Charles and me. During the days at Gordonstoun when Charles used to come to my dog-kennel room to look at television, there was an Associated-Rediffusion series *The Life and Times of Lord Mountbatten*, I think it was called: something like that. It would have taken a pack of wolves to keep him away from the set when that was showing. He was absolutely fascinated by it. To see a whole series of programmes devoted to his great-uncle must have made an enormous impression on the boy. No wonder he was so intensely attracted to his 'Uncle Dickie'.

I was with him on a few occasions when he went to visit Lord Mountbatten at his home, Broadlands, at Romsey in Hampshire. I'm sure they were among his happiest times, like those when he visited Queen Elizabeth The Queen

Mother. Both she and 'Uncle Dickie' always had two precious gifts to give him: time and attention. Although their lists of official duties were heavy, they did not compare with those of Charles's parents, and they could be leisurely with him. At Broadlands Charles and Lord Mountbatten spent hours walking in the grounds together. His influence on Charles was very strong, and the awful death from a terrorist's bomb in August, 1979 of one of the very few people with whom the Prince had such empathy must have been a shattering blow to the young man. Mountbatten had an irreplaceable part in his life.

Epilogue: Wales…and the Short Goodbye

There used to be a very well-worn cliché in old TV thrillers. The detective sergeant was with his constable assistant, or the sheriff with his sidekick when the dialogue went something like:

'What's worrying you, sergeant/sheriff? It's pretty quiet.'

'Yes, it's quiet…*too* quiet. I don't like it.'

This situation happened to me once with Prince Charles.

The first act of the story took place in November 1967. An official announcement was made that Charles would go to University College of Wales at Aberystwyth for the summer term in 1969 to learn Welsh, just before his investiture as Prince of Wales. (This seemed to me a rather unnecessary gesture, since the majority of the Welsh people don't speak the language themselves.) The announcement was greeted with less than enthusiasm by certain Welsh nationalists, and not all of them extremists.

The following summer Charles decided to spend the long vacation making a number of visits to Government departments and industrial sites, including a North Sea oil rig and a mine. He also visited the Welsh Office in Cardiff.

On that day I was with Prince Andrew and Prince Edward in London, and later at Windsor. Chief Superintendent Perkins accompanied Charles to Wales and co-operated with the local police. Maybe he thought I wouldn't be up to handling any incidents that arose, or maybe he simply wanted to get first-hand experience of the general situation in Wales in view of Charles's proposed course at Aberystwyth..

In the event, the Cardiff trip turned out to be marred by some unpleasant and some childish incidents – smoke bombs set off, eggs thrown and insulting remarks shouted, things of that nature. I was told afterwards that Charles was baffled much more than scared: he simply couldn't understand why the demonstrations were directed against him, for he had no illwill for Wales or the people. He left his group and went to the barrier and spoke to some of the noisier protesters to get a rational explanation of their point of view. He was greeted with vulgar abuse and childish jibes. Eventually Charles got fed up and walked away.

In going over to the protesters Charles showed that he was politically imprudent but as courageous as ever. From what I could gather later, that impressed some of the less rabid demonstrators.

When he was back in London and we had joined up again, he again mentioned how perplexed he was by it all, his face screwed up in the familiar puzzled expression. 'I simply wanted to know what the protest was about, but I just got abuse. Finally I gave it up. There was no point.'

A few months later he returned to Cardiff to chair the first meeting of the Welsh Committee, and this time I went as his protection officer. I was keyed up – as much as my normally placid temperament could manage – expecting something like Prince Charles's last trip. Although I didn't think I should have to do much more than field a few eggs or kick away a smoke-bomb there was always the possibility of one hot-head's doing something really stupid – with the best of motives, of course.

As we approached the Welsh Office I could see there was a hefty contingent of local police on duty. But instead of a noisy crowd with incomprehensible (to English-speakers) banners, there were at best half a dozen members of the public near the entrance, and they were apathetic enough.

'It looks pretty quiet,' Prince Charles observed, rather surprised.

I very nearly said, 'I don't like it. It's too quiet.' I stopped in time, to avoid worrying Charles and, more importantly, to avoid sounding foolish. And yet it was worrying, all that quiet, when we had expected a noisy, unfriendly greeting.

I didn't feel really comfortable until we were on our way home again, and when I thought of his forthcoming term at Aberystwyth the comfortable feeling drained away. I assumed that I should be accompanying him there. This assumption was reinforced by an invitation to lunch from Dr Glyn Daniel, who accompanied us on the France and Jersey trip, at which he planned to brief me on the general mood of the town and mark up a map for me. In the event I did not go to Aberystwyth with Charles.

During Charles's last term at Trinity to my considerable surprise I had a visit from Chief Superintendent Perkins, which was rather like the mountain coming to Mahomet's assistant. While Charles was attending a lecture Perkins visited me in my room. He told me that Detective Sergeant Tony Speed would be taking over as Charles's protection officer when he returned to Cambridge. I was totally taken aback. As I have said, when I first became the Prince's personal detective, I was warned that the duty would be for only three months to avoid his becoming too dependent on one man. The authorities – which included the royal family, I assume – didn't want a repetition of the emotional upset caused by Don Green's departure after the cherry brandy incident. So, at every significant stage of his life I was expecting to be told that I should be posted away from him. As the months, and then more than six years passed that unhappy expectation gradually diminished.

So when at last I was told that my duty was ending, it came as a severe shock, a much greater one than the news of my original appointment. As soon as I gathered my thoughts I asked whether Charles wanted to be rid of me.

'No, he'd like to have you stay on.'

'So why...?'

'It's felt that Prince Charles should have a more senior officer.'

There was no answer to that.

I had also been told when I first became Charles's protection officer that when the job was over I could choose whatever branch of the service I wanted to go in. After I had got over the initial shock, I told Perkins I should like to go into Special Branch. The answer came back:

'Sorry, no vacancies.'

I thought again. 'I'd like to join CID.'

'Sorry, no vacancies.'

I tried again later. 'The Planning Department.'

'Sorry, no vacancies.'

To his great credit, there is no doubt that Chief Superintendent Perkins did everything he could for me, but the 'No vacancies' decisions were taken by The People Upstairs. Finally the Chief Superintendent suggested that I go back to ordinary duties and take the promotion examination. When I was promoted Charles would have me back, because he had said he wanted me back; he didn't want to lose me.

'So if I do go back to general duties and get my promotion, what guarantee will I have that I'll get my old job back?'

'I'm sorry: you should know better than that. No one can give any guarantees in the service.'

At last I decided to write an end to this chapter of my life and resign from the Metropolitan Police. After what I had experienced in the Royal Protection Group anything else risked being an anti-climax.

On 22 June 1969 I became a civilian, but at the last moment Chief Superintendent Perkins told me that I should keep 27 June free because Prince Charles wanted to see me to say goodbye officially.

As I walked through the gate of Buckingham Palace, past the uniformed policeman on duty, it seemed only yesterday that I had been stationed there myself, charged with the undemanding sheepdog task of keeping out tourists. And yet it also seemed an age, so much had happened since that first day. I had spent by far the greater part of seven years with twenty-four-hours-a-day responsibility for the safety of the heir to the throne. I had been at his side from the days when he was an unhappy, lonely and slightly podgy boy until he had grown into a serious and handsome young man who had learned to carry the terrible weight of his inescapable life-sentence with dignity and fortitude. He still had a strong strain of shyness and self-deprecation in his make-up, but he had become far more resolute: he was much more his own man and when he wanted to do something, he did it. Only his parents – and not always even they? – could make him do something he didn't want to do.

Someone at Buckingham Palace once pointed out to me rather severely that it had been a great privilege for me to be so close to the Prince of Wales for so long. I was aware of it; and I was proud that I had helped him in his formative years, that I had been someone he could rely on and ask for advice, particularly during those first unhappy years at Gordonstoun.

Charles was by nature a highly complex and basically introverted figure of many contradictions, yet in one respect at least he was positive and uncomplicated: in his unwavering sense of duty and responsibility. Yes, it was a great privilege, but for my part I had done my utmost to fulfil my duty to him and to merit that privilege. Perhaps it is not insufferably immodest of me to say that maybe my efforts did not go unnoticed, for I remained Charles's protection officer longer than any other detective before or since.

I took my time on my walk along the corridors and up the stairs towards Charles's office. I was resigned to the fact that this was probably the last time I should set foot in Buckingham Palace and I wanted to make the most of each last moment. While I waited in the ante-room to be called in to Charles I suddenly and unaccountably became nervous, even though during my years as his protection officer I had probably spent more time with him than anyone else, including his parents.

I also had an illogical half-hope that somehow our meeting would produce a reprieve, that somehow a way had been worked out for me to keep my job, even though I was now a civilian. As I walked into Charles's office he was seated at his desk, his back to the door. He rose, turned and held out his hand. We shook hands. For me, at least, it was a highly emotional moment. Charles had been the centre of seven years of my life: everything I had done revolved around him. He was the person – apart from my own mother – whom I knew best of all.

I was a little like the drowning man who is supposed to see all his life pass before his eyes in his last moments. It was not as dramatic as that, but a number of unrelated incidents flashed through my mind.

Charles asked me why I was leaving the police. To answer

him fully would have taken a long, long time, so I contented myself with saying that I thought that it was for the best in the circumstances. Charles obviously understood the reason for my evasion, or at least, that it was an evasion. He asked what I was going to do. In effect, I replied that I was going to take some time off, sit down and rethink my life. Charles gave me his best wishes for the future.

He turned to his desk and took a framed, signed photograph from a number he had there and offered it to me as a token of appreciation of what I had done for him.

There was nothing more to be said, except 'Goodbye'. I left Buckingham Palace for the last time.

For me it was a sad, slightly sour parting – at least for the moment. I felt rather let down. I suppose I thought that 6½ years' close, loyal service deserved better than a stand-up handshake and a signed photograph that appeared to be one of many that were being handed out that morning.

When I got home I went through some of my souvenirs and the correspondence I had received during my time with the Prince of Wales. Almost the first piece of paper I came across was a memorandum from 'The Equerry to HRH the Prince of Wales to PC M.J. Varney, dated 9 December 1968.

> The Prince of Wales would very much like to give you a Christmas present to show his appreciation for all that you have done for him this year.
> Rather than a random gift, if you have something you would particularly like, up to about £4 to £5, perhaps, you would care to let me know what it is?
>
> DJC

While in the Royal Protection Group I had always used a cheap, throwaway ballpoint pen. I thought it would be pleasant to have a decent pen for once, and so I opted for that.

Unfortunately it cost £8. Later I had another note from the palace pointing out that my Christmas present had cost more than the standard amount and asking me to refund the £3 difference.

Of course, it had nothing to do with Charles, and I'm sure he didn't even know about it, but in my state of dejection at the time it only aggravated my sense of alienation. Of course, common sense and a proper sense of proportion soon returned and I saw things in true perspective.

At this final meeting I learned two things. First, neither Prince Charles nor I was good at farewells. Second, Charles had changed completely from the days when he sulked for weeks on end over 'losing' Don Green because of the cherry brandy episode. Now, when a thing was over, it was over, and that was that. He had learned that his position made that attitude inevitable and essential.

Yes, it was over.

It was not until after this final meeting with Charles that I really felt the trauma of the break from my life as his personal detective. It was no exaggeration, even if it was a cliché, to say that my service in the Royal Protection Group had taken the best years of my life, from twenty-one years of age to thirty. True, I had stayed in castles, palaces and mansions; I had moved amongst royalty and nobility; princes confided in me and trusted me; I had travelled everywhere at better than first class. Suddenly it all stopped as cruelly as if a guillotine blade had fallen.

For a long time I was at a loss, disoriented, uncertain what to do.

When at last I started to put the pieces together again I added up the balance sheet. There was the rich credit of all the marvellous experiences I had enjoyed. On the debit side, I had begun as an ordinary constable, and after nearly seven years with Prince Charles I had ended as a constable. I had carried a heavy burden of responsibility longer than anyone else in my position had done or has done since. It cost me a private life of my own; I had few close friends, none of them recent. My own leisure had been at odd, snatched hours.

I became aware that the psychological price I had to pay for the distinction of having been Charles's detective was enormous.

But it was all worth it, ten times over. That Buckingham Palace official was right: I had enjoyed a great privilege in being close to Prince Charles for so long. And there was a marvellous gift I took away with me, far more valuable even than that signed photograph.

It was the certain, proud knowledge that for a while I had helped His Royal Highness Prince Charles to grow up from boy to man; that once I was the only one he could turn to.

'Do you ever get lonely?'

Now it was my turn.

Index